THE CASTLE LECTURES
IN ETHICS, POLITICS,
AND ECONOMICS

RICHARD J. GOLDSTONE

For Humanity

Reflections of a War Crimes Investigator

With a Foreword by Sandra Day O'Connor

YALE UNIVERSITY PRESS / NEW HAVEN & LONDON

Designed by Nancy Ovedovitz and set in Scala type by Tseng Information
Systems, Inc. Printed in the United States of America.

Library of Congress Cataloging-in-Publication Data
Goldstone, Richard J., 1938–
For humanity : reflections of a war crimes investigator / Richard J. Goldstone.
p.   cm. — (Castle lectures in ethics, politics, and economics)
Includes bibliographical references and index.
ISBN 0-300-08205-3 (alk. paper)
1. War crimes—South Africa.   2. Apartheid—South Africa.   3. International
Tribunal for the Prosecution of Persons Responsible for Serious Violations of
International Humanitarian Law Committed in the Territory of the Former
Yugoslavia since 1991.   4. International Tribunal for Rwanda.   5. Goldstone,
Richard J., 1938—Career in human rights.   I. Title.   II. Series.
KTL4545 .G65   2000
341.6'9'0968—dc21   99-086021

A catalogue record for this book is available from the British Library.
The paper in this book meets the guidelines for permanence and durability of
the Committee on Production Guidelines for Book Longevity of the Council
on Library Resources.

10   9   8   7   6   5   4   3   2   1

This book began as a series of Castle Lectures delivered by Richard J. Goldstone at Yale University in 1998, as part of Yale's Program in Ethics, Politics, and Economics.

The Castle Lectures, endowed by Mr. John K. Castle, honor his ancestor, the Reverend James Pierpont, one of Yale's founders. Given by prominent public figures, the lectures are intended to promote reflection on the moral foundations of society and government and to enhance understanding of ethical issues facing individuals in our complex modern society.

For Noleen

CONTENTS

FOREWORD

Since 1991, Justice Richard J. Goldstone has been at the forefront of one of the biggest challenges facing emerging democracies today—how to address grave, systematic human rights abuses committed by leaders of the previous regime. From his experience on the Goldstone Commission investigating political violence in South Africa, to his tenure as the chief prosecutor of the International Criminal Tribunals for Yugoslavia and Rwanda, he has witnessed firsthand the difficulty of achieving accountability for crimes of mass violence.

The rule of law is generally vindicated by holding transgressors accountable for their actions through prosecution and punishment. This relatively straightforward approach becomes more complicated in certain contexts, however. In states that are changing to democracy, particularly where the previous regime may have been responsible for committing serious crimes, the new government faces a difficult choice. On the one hand, our sense of "justice" demands that the offenders be called to account for their actions. This preference for prosecution is reflected in the fact that international law allows any state to prosecute the perpetrators of the most serious crimes against humanity under the theory of universal jurisdiction. On the other hand, the need to stabilize the new democratic regime first in the short run may counsel against aggressive efforts to prosecute the perpetrators and perhaps risk a renewed cycle of retribution. In these situations, efforts to achieve accountability may focus more on acknowledgments of wrongdoing and documenting the abuses rather than on punishing specific individuals.

Emerging democracies, therefore, as well as the international community, face an enormous challenge in balancing the obligation to prosecute certain crimes against the countervailing interest in securing a peaceful and full transition to democracy by forgoing punishment. As Justice Goldstone notes, emerging democracies have chosen to strike this balance in various ways. Some countries have attempted to deal with past crimes by simply ignoring the issue, some have granted blanket amnesties, some have prosecuted the perpetrators, and some have instituted truth and reconciliation commissions designed to achieve some form of acknowledgment for the victims. And in some cases, prosecution is pursued under the auspices of international criminal tribunals.

In this book, Justice Goldstone makes an important contribution to the discussion of these complex issues. The breadth of his personal experiences in South Africa and at The Hague provides unrivaled insights into the difficult choices that face emerging democracies in dealing with the crimes of a previous regime. This book draws on those experiences to provide a firsthand exploration of the pros and cons of the two main approaches to dealing with these crimes—prosecution under international auspices and truth and reconciliation commissions.

As Martha Minow has noted in *Between Vengeance and Forgiveness,* in many ways, responding to genocide or mass atrocity with legal prosecutions is to "embrace the rule of law." The decision to pursue formal trials of Nazi leaders at Nuremberg was an effort to achieve true justice— to affirm that human behavior could be judged based on preexisting standards, and that with due process the guilty could be singled out and held accountable for their crimes without resorting to vengeance. One legacy of Nuremberg is the United Nations' establishment of the two International Criminal Tribunals, for Yugoslavia and for Rwanda. The very existence of these tribunals sends a powerful message that those who commit atrocities may be held accountable for their actions under the law. At the same time, however, as Justice Goldstone points out, these tribunals have also experienced difficulties in turning that message into reality. Simply apprehending indicted and suspected war criminals in the former Yugoslavia, some of whom remain in power, has proven to be an enormous challenge, and aggressive pursuit of these individuals risks upsetting the fragile peace. The opposite problem is confronted in Rwanda—the new government of Rwanda, headed by a Tutsi, arrested and jailed over one hundred thousand Hutus and charged them with genocide and mass murder. Aside from these difficulties, pursuing accountability for crimes such as genocide through formal legal process under the auspices of international institutions is subject to other criticisms. Chief among these are charges of politicization and selectivity.

Another approach is to grant some form of immunity in return for a peaceful transfer of power. A blanket amnesty is susceptible to the charge that it is really a grant of impunity, a charge that diminishes our sense that justice is being served. Amnesty does not necessarily undermine accountability, however. South Africa's establishment of a Truth and Reconciliation Commission is a case in point. As Justice Goldstone explains, for South Africa to change from the apartheid regime to full democracy, it was essential to acknowledge the human rights abuses that had occurred, because "to ignore the victimization of the great majority of South Africans would be a recipe for escalating enmity between the races." South Africa's Truth and Reconciliation Commission identifies its goals as "reconciliation, amnesty, reparation, and the search for truth." The commission considers "gross

violations of human rights," which include "the killing, abduction, torture or severe ill-treatment of any person." These gross violations of
human rights are limited to acts that were crimes under the apartheid
legal system, and liability extends not only to acts committed by the
apartheid regime, but also to acts committed by members of liberation
movements such as the African National Congress. Although the negotiated end to apartheid included the agreement that some form of amnesty would be available for the outgoing leaders in return for a peaceful transfer to a fully democratic society, blanket anmesties were not
given. Instead, conditional grants of amnesty have been given to those
who acknowledge their crimes by providing complete and truthful testimony regarding their actions. The commission investigates the testimony and decides whether to grant the application for amnesty. If amnesty is denied, prosecution can proceed. Perpetrators whose crimes
are deemed "disproportionately" heinous or not motivated by politics
can also be denied amnesty.

This process has several advantages. First, because the amnesties
granted under this process are not designed to exculpate the state's own
agents, but instead to expose and acknowledge the crimes of a previous regime, the process promotes truth and accountability. Second, the
focus on reconciliation and healing ensures that the process looks forward to strengthening the new democratic regime, rather than looking
backward toward retribution. Finally, the process signals a break with
the past regime and can be used to build political legitimacy for the new
regime.

But just as there are limits to the effectiveness of punishments, there
are limits to amnesty. The balance between vengeance and forgiveness
is in many ways the balance between too much forgetting and too much
remembering. Blanket amnesties risk too soon forgetting the atrocities and thereby risking their repetition. Drawn-out trials or truth commission investigations risk wallowing in the past and risking renewed

cycles of violence and vengeance. Despite the difficulties, the South African approach appears to effectively balance these two goals, encouraging public accountability without the destabilizing effects of a full-fledged trial.

As shown by Justice Goldstone, accountability can be achieved in various ways. There is no one solution that is best for all situations. Justice Goldstone's experience in grappling with these issues, not just as a philosophical matter but in the crucible of real-world application, results in a unique perspective on the question of how best to achieve accountability. The wisdom, courage, and vigor with which Justice Goldstone approached his work in prosecuting war criminals as chief prosecutor of the International Tribunals for Yugoslavia and Rwanda is reflected in the pages of this book, and the lessons he has drawn from his far-ranging experiences are invaluable to all who are interested in the pursuit of peace and justice.

SANDRA DAY O'CONNOR
Associate Justice
Supreme Court of the United States

ACKNOWLEDGMENTS

This book would not have been written but for the invitation I received during 1996 from Professor Ian Shapiro of Yale University to deliver the 1998 Castle Lectures. Preparing the lectures required me to reconsider and record many of my then recent experiences in South Africa, the Netherlands, and Rwanda. I am indebted to Professor Shapiro for his encouragement and for the friendship I have received from him. Professor Robert Burt of the Yale Law School attended the three lectures and, both then and since, has offered me important new insights and criticisms. He generously read the manuscript, again offering comments and taking issue with some of my views. He will have no difficulty in recognizing in the end result how much I benefited from his incisive and wise suggestions.

My wife, Noleen, to whom I have dedicated this book, played a crucial role in all the events. Her support, counsel, and constant companionship were indispensable to the success of the endeavors described. On many long flights she patiently wrote a diary, which was a fruitful source of reference.

My researchers at the Constitutional Court of South Africa spent much time and effort reading early drafts and making important sug-

gestions. I refer to Jacqueline Cassette, Nazreen Bawa, Thabani Ma-
suku, and Nicole Fritz. I am indebted to them all.

My friend Errol Friedmann, in his early days a journalist, spent many
hours making editorial suggestions and corrections. It was a delight to
work with him.

Finally, I would like to express my deep gratitude to John S. Covell,
editor at Yale University Press, for his encouragement and advice. Until
I received the edited manuscript from Karen Gangel, I could not have
imagined the attention to detail and the valuable advice that a fortunate
author could receive from an editor. I am greatly indebted to her for the
many substantial improvements for which she is responsible.

INTRODUCTION

Perhaps the most difficult professional decision of my career was whether to accept the invitation to become a judge in the Transvaal High Court in 1980. I was forty-one years old and involved in a successful commercial practice at the Johannesburg Bar. I had served three terms as an acting judge in 1978 and 1979 and enjoyed the work immensely. Apart from the work, I appreciated the absence of pressure, which is an inevitable consequence of life at the Bar. Nonetheless, I regarded a judicial appointment at a comparatively young age as an opportunity for a mid-career change.

The most significant aspect of my decision, however, was political. From my university days I had opposed apartheid and any form of racial discrimination, and I was now being invited to assume a position requiring me to take an oath faithfully to apply the law of the land. Many of my professional colleagues and friends have faced this same problem, and have addressed it in various ways. But this is not the appropriate place to debate the difficult issues raised by this question. Suffice it to say that I decided to accept the invitation and assume the comparatively cloistered existence that is generally associated with judicial office.

The new opportunities that came to me in consequence of that deci-

sion were as unusual as they were unexpected. Little could I have anticipated becoming involved with politically sensitive judicial inquiries in
my own country, and even less playing an important role in the transition of South Africa from an apartheid state to a democracy as well as in
the establishment of the Truth and Reconciliation Commission. That I
would become an international war crimes prosecutor would have been
quite beyond my belief.

This volume is concerned with the circumstances that led to those
opportunities and with many of the experiences that came with them.
For the most part they were the subject of the three Castle Lectures I
delivered at Yale University in April 1998. The material is largely anec-
dotal and has not been recorded elsewhere. But the important events
associated with these years should, in my opinion, become part of the
public historical record. Some lessons may be learned from them—
lessons concerning the importance of prosecutors and judges remaining independent of political interference, and lessons concerning the
power of political leaders to bring about radical changes in their societies. And then there are perhaps larger lessons illustrating how a decent and credible institutional base can bring out the best in people,
though a bad one can just as easily deprave the same people. Men who
did not hesitate to work as apartheid police officers, for example, served
conscientiously and loyally with the Commission of Inquiry which I led
from 1991 to 1994 . The commission brought out their innate sense of
justice and best impulses.

I have recorded my experiences chronologically. The introductory
chapter explains how I came to be involved in the events I describe in
the succeeding pages. I then relate some of the incidents leading to
the public disclosure of the criminal conduct that accompanied South
Africa's transition to democracy, especially the conduct of some of the
most senior police officers. Thereafter I consider some of my experiences as the first prosecutor of the United Nations Criminal Tribunals

for the former Yugoslavia and Rwanda and their relevance with regard to the establishment of a permanent international criminal court.

As will emerge from these pages, I have been privileged to view political processes from the inside, yet without being one of the insiders and without having to surrender any independence or freedom of action. Few people have had that opportunity.

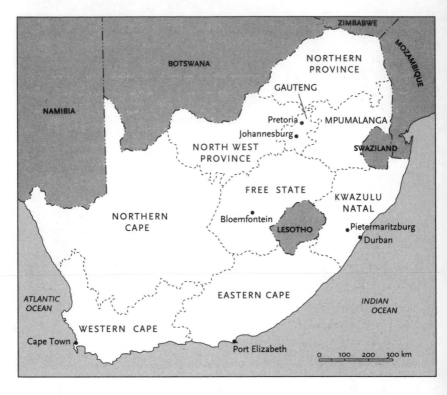

Map of South Africa Subsequent to South Africa's first democratic elections in 1994, nine new provinces replaced the original four. Sebokeng and Boipatong, sites of infamous preelection massacres, are situated in Gauteng, as is Vlakplaas, home to a notorious unit of the South African Security Police.

Map of the Former Yugoslavia The war that broke out in Bosnia-Herzegovina in March 1992 called for innovative humanitarian measures on the part of the international community. The Security Council responded by establishing the first international criminal tribunal, situated in The Hague. Recently the tribunal indicted officials for atrocities committed during the Kosovo conflict.

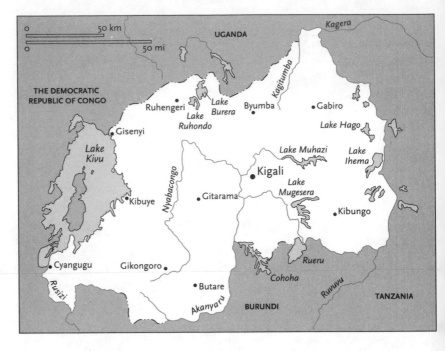

Map of Rwanda Arusha, site of the United Nations Tribunal for Rwanda, is situated in Tanzania, approximately four hundred miles southeast of Kigali, the capital of Rwanda. A location outside Rwanda was chosen to best guarantee the safety of personnel, witnesses, and those being prosecuted. The Office of the Prosecutor, however, was established in Kigali.

New Challenges: Judging Injustice

After serving twenty-seven years of a life term for high treason, Nelson Mandela was released from prison on Sunday, 11 February 1990. A few weeks earlier, the South African Police had arrested Clayton Sizwe Sithole, a soldier of Umkhonto we Sizwe (the armed wing of the African National Congress) who was also the boyfriend of Zindzi Mandela (the daughter of Nelson and Winnie Mandela) and the father of her three-month-old son. On Tuesday, 30 January 1990, four days after his arrest, Sithole was found hanged in a prison cell in the Johannesburg Central Police Station.

My role as an investigator began the following day, when I was appointed by President Frederick W. de Klerk to conduct a judicial inquiry into the cause of Sithole's death. This appointment was highly unusual, as inquests into unnatural deaths were invariably held by a magistrate, under legislation that regulated autopsies. Also unusual was the appointment of a person who had had little previous experience of criminal procedures or investigations. My expertise lay in the commercial field. The decision to appoint a judge of what was then the highest court in the land to inquire into this matter reflected the political sensitivity of the incident.

By 1990 almost one hundred people had died in police detention. In every case the police put out exculpatory explanations. Some of the detainees had "slipped on a piece of soap," thereby sustaining fatal head injuries. Others had suffered "acute depression" after having given information concerning their friends and had "committed suicide" by jumping out of upper-floor windows of a police building. Never was there an admission of police brutality or torture as the cause. The most publicized of such deaths was undoubtedly that of Steve Biko, the leader of the Black Consciousness Movement and a popular figure in South Africa's black community. Only recently, in their amnesty applications to South Africa's Truth and Reconciliation Commission, have five police officers admitted that they fatally assaulted Biko while he was in their custody. Regardless of the explanations offered, however, there was a widespread assumption that the police were responsible for deaths in detention, and this made the alleged suicide of Sithole all the more sensitive.

As the evidence unfolded during five days of oral testimony, it became clear beyond any question that Sithole had in fact taken his own life; indeed, it was accepted by the legal team acting for his family. I found that one of the probable reasons for the suicide was remorse at having informed the police of alleged criminal conduct by both Winnie and Zindzi Mandela. Because Winnie Mandela was not represented at the inquiry, I considered it unfair for the substance of those allegations to be made public. With the agreement of counsel for the Sithole family and the South African Police, the allegations were kept confidential.

Shortly after the Sithole inquiry, I became involved in the investigation of the causes of violence in South Africa during its transition from apartheid to democracy. As a direct consequence I was appointed the first Chief Prosecutor of the United Nations International Criminal Tribunals for the former Yugoslavia and Rwanda, a formal title for the dual role of war crimes investigator and prosecutor.

When I travel abroad, the question I am most frequently asked is "Why you?" The answer requires me to go back to my student days at the University of the Witwatersrand. There I had the opportunity to meet blacks among my fellow students and developed a deep sense of the injustice they were forced to endure in their daily lives. When I returned to a comfortable home in a white suburb, those students went to the squalor of the black townships. Because many of their homes had no electricity, they had no option but to study at night by the poor illumination of paraffin lamps or, in some cases, candles.

Within months of my first year's study, my sense of shame and injustice caused me to become active in student organizations. They were then fighting a battle against the proposed introduction by the government of apartheid structures within the few South African universities that admitted students of color. I was elected to the Students' Representative Council and soon thereafter to the executive committee of the National Union of South African Students (NUSAS).

In 1957 I represented NUSAS at meetings of World University Service (WUS) in West Africa. My codelegate was Jeffrey Jowell, later to become the dean of the law school at University College, London, and the coauthor, with Lord Harry Woolf, of the leading English textbook on administrative law. It was the first time I had traveled abroad, and what a delight and privilege it was to meet students and faculty from scores of countries around the world. It was also my first experience of the cohesion and commitment of the international student antiapartheid movement. That I was welcomed, and literally embraced, by students from other African countries was an emotional experience. It was also a strong reminder of the life all South Africans could then have enjoyed in a free, democratic, and nonracist society. But, alas, that was still thirty-seven years in the making.

My student leadership days also brought me into unsolicited contact with the security police. They were particularly interested in student activists, and many days and nights I was followed by unfriendly plain-clothes police in Volkswagens. They made their presence obvious in an attempt to frighten and harass people whose activities they disapproved of. Of course, it did not have that effect—indeed, to young, otherwise carefree students, their activities lent added excitement to our whole endeavor. My parents, I recall, did not share this laissez-faire attitude—but, to their credit, they did not pressure me to cease my activities.

NUSAS and the Students' Representative Council also brought me into contact with some of the leaders of the antiapartheid movement in South Africa at that time. We used to have monthly meetings at the home of Bishop Ambrose Reeves, the Anglican bishop of Johannes-burg. There, we were joined by representatives of thirteen other organi-zations, which included the African National Congress (ANC), the Con-gress of Democrats, and the South African Indian Congress. I shared with them their dreams of a South Africa in which all people would live in harmony as equal citizens of the country of their birth.

My student activism lasted for the first four years of my six-year law degree. In the last two years I worked as a candidate attorney for the large commercial firm of Edward Nathan and Friedland in Johannes-burg. In the late afternoons I would attend law lectures at Witwaters-rand University Law School. In December 1962, within weeks of gradu-ating, I married Noleen Behrman, whom I had met on the steps of the university when she was playing hooky from a psychology experiment, having become frustrated because the rats were running the wrong way. All but one, as it turned out!

◇   ◇   ◇

Since the nineteenth century, South Africa has had a dual Bar based on the English model, with barristers and solicitors. From my earliest school days it had been my ambition to become a barrister, and I began my practice at the Johannesburg Bar in April 1963. Although the combination of my family commitments and my law practice kept me out of active politics, I became an interested observer, increasingly frustrated and full of despair at the enforcement of laws designed to impose apartheid in greater and greater measure and to snuff out opposition to those policies.

I built a successful commercial practice and in 1977 was appointed as a senior counsel (the equivalent of Queen's Counsel in England). According to South African tradition, superior court judges were appointed from the ranks of senior counsel. To make good its boast of having an independent judiciary, successive apartheid governments elevated some barristers to the High Court Bench notwithstanding any active opposition to government policies on their part.

In 1978 I was offered an acting appointment as a judge on the Transvaal Supreme Court. The moral problems of joining the South African judiciary were manifest. Its members were obliged, by their oaths of office, to enforce the laws of the land. This was a great concern to me. I decided, however, that I could play a more active role in efforts to ameliorate those laws by accepting the appointment rather than by continuing to pursue a lucrative commercial career. Leaders of the Johannesburg Bar who were themselves antiapartheid activists encouraged me to accept the appointment. The drop in income was appreciable, but, as she has done throughout my career, Noleen supported my decision. Little did we anticipate the exciting years that lay ahead!

I accepted a permanent appointment to the Transvaal Supreme Court in August 1980. An early opinion I delivered in November 1982 brought national and international attention. It related to the laws through which residential segregation had been enforced since 1950.

The statute, known as the Group Areas Act, had been amended and updated in 1966. The legislation empowered the government to decree that certain areas of South Africa were to be reserved for the exclusive use of people of one or another color. It was a criminal offense for a person of the "wrong" color to reside or own property in such a group area. The most desirable areas were set aside for whites, and the least desirable for blacks. Some areas were set aside for Asians, and some areas for "coloreds" (people of mixed descent). The opinion was delivered in an appeal of the conviction of a Mrs. Govender, an elderly Asian woman, on a charge of unlawfully residing with her children and grandchildren in a rented house in a part of Johannesburg reserved for whites.

When Mrs. Govender appeared before a magistrate, she pleaded guilty and was sentenced to a fine of less than ten dollars or to fifteen days' imprisonment, all of which was suspended for three years on the condition that she not be convicted of a similar offense during that time. However, the sting was an order that she be ejected from the home. What was unusual in this case was that Mrs. Govender's counsel had persuaded the magistrate to suspend the ejectment order for nine months. He did so on the strength of evidence which established that there were no alternative accommodations for Asians in the Johannesburg area, that Mrs. Govender had been on a waiting list for some seven years, and that she might have to wait another ten before such accommodations would become available. Mrs. Govender appealed to the Transvaal High Court only on the grounds that the magistrate should have suspended the order indefinitely or until she found alternative accommodations.

A two-judge panel, comprising Judge Louis le Grange and me, heard the appeal. In a discussion before hearing argument, we had come to the conclusion that we were not able to assist Mrs. Govender. During the oral argument, however, a new approach occurred to me. At my request, we adjourned early for lunch so that I could discuss the new point with my colleague. Over lunch and a glass of wine, I pointed out that the Group Areas Act of 1966 provided that a court convicting a person for living in a "wrong" group area "may . . . make an order for the ejectment" of such person. In contrast, the original 1950 statute provided that the court "shall" make such an order. We agreed that since the promulgation of the 1966 amendment, courts had failed to pay attention to the fact that the power to make an ejectment order had become discretionary. When the hearing resumed, I requested counsel to consider the effect of the change in the wording of the provision, resulting in a two-week adjournment. In the subsequent judgment we set aside the ejectment order. In the course of my opinion, I said that

> The power to make such an ejectment order is a wide one. It is one which may, and in most cases will, seriously affect the lives of the person or persons concerned. It may, and frequently will, interfere with the normal contractual relationship which exists between landlord and tenant. Such an order should not therefore be made without the fullest enquiry. . . .
>
> The prosecutor, if requested by an interested party to seek such an order, would be obliged to place material before the court to justify the exercise of the court's discretion to grant the ejectment order. I cannot imagine any circumstances which would justify a court making such an order *mero motu* [of its own accord]. Many considerations may be relevant to the exercise of the court's discretion.[1]

One of a number of considerations to which I referred was "the personal hardship which such an order may cause and the availability of alternative accommodation."

Little could I have imagined that this opinion would bring to an immediate stop all prosecutions under the Group Areas Act. It had become politically embarrassing for the government to make the issue of an ejectment order peremptory, and prosecutors were unable to establish the availability of alternative accommodations. In consequence, substantial areas of the larger cities of South Africa became "mixed" in the years that followed the Govender decision.

A few years later, as an item on the order paper (a list of questions that members of Parliament put to government ministers), Gaye Derby-Lewis, a right-wing member of Parliament, asked the president, then P. W. Botha, why the government was allowing "blacks" to reside in "white areas." Botha, somewhat disingenuously, replied that the government had no alternative because of "a judgment of Judge Goldstone." She asked whether the country was being run by the government or Judge Goldstone! This incident had a sequel in 1993, to which I will return in Chapter 2.

In 1986, another case received publicity, this one involving seizure by the security police of calendars printed on behalf of the Release Mandela Campaign, an association dedicated to freeing Nelson Mandela. The calendars contained the preamble to the Freedom Charter, an ANC charter passed at the Congress of the People in 1956, four years before that organization was declared unlawful under the security laws that were introduced in the wake of the deaths of sixty-nine protesters in Sharpeville. The calendar highlighted the birthdates of Nelson Mandela and Walter Sisulu[2] and recorded the dates of Steve Biko's and Neil Aggett's deaths during police detention, as well as the dates of the Sharpeville Massacre and Uitenhage Massacre.[3] The police justified the seizure of the calendars, inter alia, on the grounds that their contents would further the activities of a banned organization, namely, the African National Congress. I set aside the seizure of the calendars and ordered that they be returned to the Release Mandela Campaign. I did so on the strength of the evidence of Dr. Tom Lodge, a senior lecturer in political studies from the University of the Witwatersrand. He testified that the terms of the Freedom Charter mirrored the principles to be found in the Universal Declaration of Human Rights and other human rights conventions and were accepted as the norm in the United States of America and most western European nations. It followed, too, a recent decision of two colleagues in the Transvaal Supreme Court who concluded that demands for the release of Nelson Mandela had become so widespread that they could no longer be identified solely with the ANC.

For more than three years, from 1985 to 1989, South Africa was governed by emergency laws proclaimed by President Botha. They allowed for the detention of a person without trial if the police considered that detention "necessary for the maintenance of public order or the safety of the public or that person himself, or for the termination of the state of emergency." The detention period of up to fourteen days could be extended indefinitely by the minister of law and order. At one point in 1986, some ten thousand South Africans were being held in prisons and police cells under these emergency regulations.

From the time of my appointment to the Transvaal Supreme Court, I had exercised the power given to all South African judges to visit prisons. Unfortunately, not many of my colleagues shared this interest or regarded such visits as a duty. Judicial visits were allowed only to individuals held in the regular prisons, not to those detained in police cells. And, of course, it was in police cells that third-degree methods and torture took place.

Toward the end of 1985, Botha requested in Parliament that judges be permitted to visit people being held in prisons and police cells under the emergency regulations. Although he gave no reasons for the request, he was subtly but unquestionably sending a message to prison and police authorities not to assault or torture detainees. It was also a way of reassuring South Africans and the international community that detainees, many of whom were children, would not be physically ill treated.

Shortly thereafter, I was approached by Wes Boshoff, the judge-president of the Transvaal Supreme Court, who asked if I would be willing to take off six months from my court duties. During that time he wanted me to visit detainees held in prisons and police cells in the Transvaal Province. He was aware of my interest in prisoners and prison conditions and my long association with the National Institute for Crime Prevention and Rehabilitation of Offenders (NICRO) as chairperson and later president.

The approach from the judge-president immediately created a serious dilemma for me. I did not believe the judiciary should become involved in a system that detained people without trial—a system abhorrent to anyone who respected fundamental human rights. At the same time, I recognized that the detainees would probably benefit from the protection a visiting judge could give to them.

I decided to seek advice from a longtime friend, George Bizos, a member of the Johannesburg Bar and for many years the adviser of both Nelson and Winnie Mandela. Bizos had been involved in a number of autopsies related to deaths in detention. He immediately understood my conflict and advised me to visit some detainees and find out what they wished me to do. Acting on his advice, I went to the police station in the city center and requested access to the detainees. Despite the police officers' surprise at my request, I was given a doctor's consulting room as my office. The first detainee I spoke to was Zwelakhe Sisulu, the son of Walter Sisulu and, like his father, a leading member of the ANC. At the time he was the editor of *New Nation,* the weekly newspaper he produced on behalf of the South African Catholic Bishops' Conference. Mr. Sisulu's complaints were serious: he had been kept for some weeks in isolation; the lights in his cell were kept on twenty-four hours a day; and a closed-circuit television camera recorded his movements day and night. He had been given no reading material—not even the Bible, which the regulations mandated for every detainee.

After I had listened to Sisulu's grievances, I told him that I wanted some advice from him. I remember how he put his head back and gave a deep laugh. He said it was rich having a Supreme Court judge ask a detainee for advice. I assured him that I was serious and told him of my dilemma. He immediately grasped the issue and without hesitation said, "I am so pleased to see you. Please come back soon. That will be the attitude also of the other detainees." That ended my equivocation, and later that afternoon I informed the judge-president that I would do as he had requested. I spent the next six months visiting hundreds of detainees. After that period, my assignment continued on a part-time basis, and I visited detainees in the Transvaal Province for another eighteen months, until the emergency laws came to an end.

The original emergency laws were draconian. Detainees were not allowed to consult with lawyers, and it was an offense for any person to disclose not only the whereabouts of a detainee but also the fact that the person in question had been detained. Detainees were not allowed to receive visits from family members, a particularly harsh restriction, as many detainees were children, some as young as eleven. Within a few weeks I was able to convince the minister of law and order to allow detainees to receive regular visits from their families. Applications for such visits necessitated a visit to the local police station, the completion of a form, and the issue of a written permit. I also introduced a system whereby detainees were able to receive magazines—on the condition that they be approved by the head of the prison or the police cells. Over the following years I collected many thousands of magazines for distribution. For reasons never explained to me, however, the minister was set against detainees' having any books other than the Bible.

During those two and a half years, I visited more than three thousand people being detained without trial. It was soul-destroying work. None of them had committed any criminal offense, and some had been incarcerated for more than two years. Most were politically active in their own communities and were involved in the struggle against the apartheid government. It is difficult to imagine the mental agony of being kept in prison indefinitely. Many thought they had been forgotten and would never be set free. Under those circumstances, it is not difficult to appreciate the importance of my visits.

Much of my work consisted in convincing unsympathetic police officers to adopt a more humane attitude toward the detainees. As far as many of the police officers were concerned, those detained were enemies of the state and hardly deserving of sympathy. At one prison near Johannesburg, where many hundreds of detainees were being kept, I discovered that none had received a visit from a family member. Some of the detainees informed me that the problem lay in the requirement that a visiting permit had to be obtained from the local police station. Family members were scared to be seen there for fear of being branded police informers. I was able to convince a sympathetic local police chief that a different system had to be introduced. He agreed that the solution was to have NICRO social workers meet the family members at a local church, where the required police forms were completed. The NICRO workers then delivered them to the police station and later returned with the visiting permits. Through this system, many thousands of prison visits were made possible.

By 1989, the third year of the state of emergency, the mental state of many of the detainees had deteriorated. What had begun as frustration often developed into depression. At the end of a several-day visit to the Johannesburg Prison, I assembled all the detainees in the dining hall and asked if they wished to raise any further matters with me. I recall a young ANC activist, Seth Mazibuko, raising his hand. He reminded me that the detainees had all refused to wear prison clothes and were allowed only one set of their own clothes at a time. "Judge," he said, "we have our own clothes to wear but we are tired of them. Surely there are some people outside who would like us to have new, clean track suits and running shoes." I found this a good idea and asked Mazibuko if he would send me the names of the detainees, along with their shoe and clothing sizes. Later the same day, the prison authorities delivered the list to me at court. By chance, John Pegge, the director of NICRO, was visiting my chambers. I told him that it would be appropriate for NICRO to provide the requested items. He agreed, though we were surprised by the high estimate he received from a large store in Johannesburg. NICRO certainly did not have such funds. I suggested that he ask Ismael Ayob, who for years had been the attorney of the Mandela family, to obtain a lower quotation from merchants he might represent. He did. Pegge, on his own initiative, stopped by the office of the British consul general and asked for financial assistance. The consul general gave Pegge a check for part of the amount, and Ayob made up the difference from his own pocket. The clothes were delivered to the detainees on the following day.

Of the thousands of magazines I collected and stored in our garage, many came from local and foreign journalists; I recall that Helen Suzman, an opposition member of the South African Parliament, gave me her collection of the *New Yorker*. These were particularly enjoyed by many of the detainees, especially by Zwelakhe Sisulu. I seldom had problems in obtaining the consent I needed to distribute the magazines. On one occasion, however, during 1989, I delivered a large number of magazines to a police station in Johannesburg and asked the police chief to help me carry them from my car. On top of the pile were some *Time* magazines. "I cannot allow political detainees to read *Time*," he stated. "Why not?" I inquired, somewhat puzzled. "You know, Judge," he said, with a note of conviction in his voice, "this magazine quotes people like Senator Kennedy." I could hardly deny his observation, so there was little I could say in reply. And there was no way I could have convinced him that the utterances of Ted Kennedy would not make young South African political activists more dangerous. A couple of years later I was invited to dinner by Kennedy, who enjoyed the story.

Since the first democratic elections in 1994, I have come across scores of former detainees who are eager to recount our first meeting. Some now occupy high positions in government and in the business sector.

The activities I have described may explain why I was approached to conduct the Sithole inquest and the much more complex investigations thereafter. The government was aware that I would not make findings against it without good cause, and the majority of South Africans had confidence that I would not hesitate to make findings against the government if the evidence justified it.

The first official meeting between the African National Congress and the de Klerk government to consider a negotiated transition for South Africa was to have been held on 31 March 1990. It was postponed, however, because of what came to be called the Sebokeng Massacre. Five days earlier, a crowd of about fifty thousand ANC supporters had been marching in a township some twenty-five miles from Johannesburg. The authorities were determined to stop the march before it reached an exclusively white residential area. A line of South African Police began by blocking the crowd while it was still in the black township; the police then opened fire at the crowd using live ammunition, killing eleven and injuring more than four hundred. Mandela's response was immediate. He warned de Klerk that the government could not talk about negotiations, on the one hand, and murder "our people," on the other.

De Klerk appointed me to chair a judicial inquiry to investigate the circumstances of the shooting. By that time I had been elevated to the Supreme Court of Appeal, then known as the Appellate Division of the Supreme Court—the highest court of appeal. I accepted and decided that the hearings should be held publicly in a venue as close as possible to the scene of the shooting so as to enable the victims and their families to hear the evidence for themselves. The inquiry was facilitated by unusual video footage of the incident, which had been delivered anonymously to my chambers shortly before the public hearings were to commence. A television crew had obviously made the video, and from the friendly reaction of the crowd to the cameraman, I had little doubt that it was an American team. The tape captured the police lineup but, unfortunately, not the moment the shooting began. At that point the focus was on the demonstrators.

In investigating the incident and presenting the evidence before the commission, I was fortunate in having a young, hard-working, and highly intelligent deputy attorney general, Johan du Toit (known as "J. J."). He conceived the idea of having the video image of the police line blown up into a large photograph. He then requested that police identify each person in the line. On a given morning, all those in the photograph were told to present themselves at the scene of the shooting. J. J. then walked along the line of police officers and asked each individual to describe not only what he had done at the time of the shooting but also what those on either side of him had done. As a result, he was able to ascertain who had fired the first shot—which proved to be from a gas canister fired in panic. And that shot had caused a chain reaction. In fact no order to shoot had been given by the commanding officer. This astute investigation was especially significant in the ensuing detailed inquiry.

One individual in the photograph of the police lineup was not present for questioning. Only after some pressuring did the police authorities admit that the man, who could clearly be seen holding a revolver in his hand, was a passerby who had heard about the trouble on his car radio and had decided to help the police. This was an indication of the laxity of discipline and control even in a serious police activity of this kind.

Over the next few weeks, evidence from witnesses was submitted and was followed by detailed submissions from counsel representing interested parties. George Bizos, who had given me such wise advice with regard to detainee visits, appeared on behalf of the victims who had been injured by the bullets and of the families of those killed. My finding was that the police had acted unlawfully when they opened fire on the demonstrators and that those responsible should be prosecuted for murder and culpable homicide. Prosecutions followed, but the criminal trial came to an end when the policemen applied to the Truth and Reconciliation Commission for amnesty. The government, however, paid substantial amounts in civil claims to the victims and survivors.

The report into the Sebokeng shooting led to my first experience with hate mail and threatening telephone calls at odd hours of the day and night. I was grateful that by this time our two daughters were no longer living at home. Our elder daughter, Glenda, was married and our younger daughter, Nicole, was living in Israel. Noleen never complained, and neither of us allowed threats to our lives or security to change the way we lived, even though I now looked at everything going on around me a bit more suspiciously. In subsequent years the security risks became more serious.

The Sebokeng Massacre was the first of many serious incidents of violence and intimidation that eroded the euphoria surrounding the negotiation process that had gripped South Africa after Mandela's release. It was replaced by an atmosphere of realism. Soon, however, the whole peace process was jeopardized by the ongoing political violence that was claiming so many lives. On 14 September 1991, the major parties and personalities involved in the peace process attended a meeting at a Johannesburg hotel and set up a National Peace Accord. It was attended by about fifty political, church, business, and civic groups from all over the country. According to the terms of the Peace Accord, peace committees were established in every city, town, and village in South Africa.

Some months before the National Peace Accord was negotiated, the de Klerk government had piloted a statute through Parliament which made provision for the appointment, by the president, of a Standing Commission of Inquiry Regarding the Prevention of Public Violence and Intimidation. Governments had not infrequently appointed judges to head inquiries into specific incidents—especially politically sensitive ones. But a standing judicial commission of inquiry was something new. What was also unusual was that in addition to the usual power to summon witnesses before the commission, the statute conferred upon the chairperson the power to order officials of the commission to search and seize documents or any object at any premises in the country. In terms of the statute, the chairperson was to be assisted by four other members. The African National Congress and its allies, however, were not prepared to be associated with a commission of inquiry appointed by de Klerk. A compromise was reached whereby de Klerk agreed that he would make appointments of the chairperson and members of the commission only with the unanimous support of all of the parties to the National Peace Accord.

Toward the end of October 1991, I was informed by Kobie Coetsee, the minister of justice, that the parties to the National Peace Accord had unanimously agreed that I should be invited to head the commission. I entertained grave doubts and misgivings concerning such an appointment. My decision was not made easier when Coetsee warned me that, given the political ramifications of the appointment, I might well have to leave the Bench. To the extent that the government could commit itself for the future, it would seek to ensure that my career would not be compromised, and as a possible solution he suggested a diplomatic career. It was also obvious that accepting this appointment would have substantial impact on Noleen and me, though it was simply not possible to anticipate what that effect would be. In less than twenty-four hours I accepted what was clearly a great challenge and responsibility. For the next three years, the commission, which came to be known as the Goldstone Commission, conducted over forty major investigations. Some of them produced the first hard evidence of the involvement of the security forces in what came to be called "third force" activities, which were specifically intended to abort the peace process in South Africa.

In 1992 the political negotiations in South Africa became deadlocked, and the secretary-general of the United Nations, Boutros Boutros-Ghali, sent Cyrus Vance to South Africa as his representative. Vance, the former secretary of state in the Carter administration, set up an office in the Carlton Hotel in Johannesburg. I was requested to meet with him on a Monday morning to brief him on the work of my commission. On the day before the meeting I had read in a newspaper that Vance had canceled his attendance at a Sunday morning church service in Boipatong, a black township near Johannesburg. A few weeks before, a particularly callous and murderous group of people had rampaged through Boipatong and indiscriminately murdered and injured scores of innocent men, women, and children — an incident that caused the ANC to walk out of the negotiation process. Vance had changed his mind based on the opinion of the government that it would be unsafe for him to visit the township. I had no doubt that he had been given incorrect advice.

After discussion of commission business, Vance asked for my opinion on his decision not to attend the church service in Boipatong. I told him frankly that I thought he had acted on unfortunate advice. When he wondered what might be done to rectify the misunderstanding, I told him he should make a point of being seen in black townships and not give the impression that his visit to South Africa consisted only of meetings in a city hotel. He concurred and asked if I would arrange such visits and also accompany him. I agreed to do so on the condition that the visits be informal and private.

I immediately contacted the leader of the ANC in the area, Tokyo Sexwale, who later became the first democratically elected premier of Gauteng Province. At my request he accompanied Cy Vance and me to Boipatong. I also called Themba Khoza, the regional leader of Chief Buthelezi's Inkatha Freedom Party, who agreed that after we had completed our visit to Boipatong, he would accompany us to an Inkatha-supporting squatter camp, Crossroads, which was not far from Boipatong. It was important that Vance not be seen as favoring the ANC.

Just prior to leaving the hotel for Boipatong, Vance's United Nations assistant asked me whether I had informed the government of our proposed visit. Nothing had been further from my thoughts, I answered; and had I done so, we would undoubtedly have been accompanied by a large contingent of armed police in armored vehicles. I would not feel comfortable visiting a black township in that way and suggested that Vance felt similarly. Vance immediately intervened and said, rather sharply, that he had asked me to arrange the visit, and he was going with me.

The visit to Boipatong and Crossroads was remarkable for Vance—or so he has told me on more than one occasion since then. Within minutes of our arrival, word spread that we were there. Thousands of people converged on us, and at both stops the friendship and appreciation of the people was palpable. This warm reception came as no surprise, as I had experienced that friendship on many prior visits to black townships in various parts of South Africa. My abiding memory of that day was of the courage of Vance, who did not hesitate to act on my advice and in defiance of that given to him by the most senior members of the government.

Following closely upon the Vance visit, a report he submitted to Secretary-General Boutros-Ghali and to the Security Council commended the work of my commission. His comments were reflected in Resolution 772 of the council, dated 17 August 1992. Soon after, I received an unusual invitation to meet informally with the Security Council in New York in order to brief its members on the state of violence then plaguing South Africa. Little could I have anticipated that the next time I briefed the Security Council, it would be as an official of the United Nations.

In April 1994 South Africa held its first democratic elections. The ANC received a convincing majority, and in the following month Nelson Mandela was inaugurated as president. The ceremony, held at the Union Buildings in Pretoria, was attended by tens of thousands of South Africans in the presence of heads of state and royalty from well over one hundred countries. I would certainly count it as one of the most exciting days of my life. With the newly elected government in power, the work of the Goldstone Commission effectively came to an end. Formally, the commission continued until the end of its three-year term, which expired at the end of October 1994.

In May 1993 the Security Council established the International Criminal Tribunal for the former Yugoslavia; its seat was to be The Hague, the capital city of the Netherlands. Eleven judges were appointed to the tribunal in September of that year. In the following month the Security Council, on the nomination of the secretary-general, appointed the then attorney general of Venezuela, Ramon Escovar-Salom, as the chief prosecutor of the tribunal. He arrived at The Hague during January 1994, but within a few days he resigned to take an appointment as his country's minister of the interior. A new prosecutor had to be appointed by the Security Council, but its various members vetoed eight nominees of the secretary-general during the next five months. The whole future and credibility of the tribunal had become seriously jeopardized.

Late in June 1994, Antonio Cassese, an Italian who had been appointed president of the Yugoslavia tribunal, and Roger Arrera, a judge of the French Conseil d'Etat, met at a seminar on human rights. Cassese expressed the concern of the judges at the continuing failure by the Security Council to appoint a chief prosecutor. Frustrated and angry, the judges had completed the laborious task of drafting the rules of procedure and evidence for the tribunal and were waiting to begin their work. Without a chief prosecutor, however, the investigations themselves could not begin. Indictments and trials were therefore many months away. Arrera suggested to Cassese that I be considered as a candidate for the position. Soon after the Goldstone Commission began its work, I had met and become friendly with Arrera during an official visit to Paris to study French police methods of crowd control.

At the beginning of July 1994, I returned from a European vacation and found a fax from Cassese inquiring as to whether I would be interested in the position of chief prosecutor of the Yugoslavia tribunal. I was surprised at what I regarded as a most unusual invitation. Although I had read of the establishment of the tribunal, I knew little about it. Furthermore, I had no knowledge of humanitarian law and had never before acted as a prosecutor. My initial inclination to decline the invitation was overtaken by Noleen's strong wish to get away from the tension of our lives in South Africa. I decided that before making a final decision, I should seek the advice of Cy Vance. After Vance's visit to South Africa, the secretary-general had appointed him as his special representative in the former Yugoslavia. (As a South African I selfishly regretted that appointment because, in my opinion, had Vance remained engaged in South Africa, the negotiated death of apartheid would have been hastened.) I called Vance in New York, and he unhesitatingly and persuasively urged me to become the chief prosecutor in The Hague.

As a judge of the Supreme Court of Appeal, it would have been inappropriate for me to accept a position with the United Nations without consulting the government. I decided to discuss the matter with Dullah Omar, who had become the minister of justice following Coetsee. He informed me that the government had decided to offer me a seat on the new Constitutional Court. Few lawyers would not regard that privilege as the pinnacle of his or her career, and I was not prepared to give up the opportunity. At that time Mandela had recently appointed Arthur Chaskalson as the president of the Constitutional Court. Until 1994, South Africa had had no written constitution, and the courts no power of judicial review. Parliament was supreme. Because the ANC considered the credibility of a new Supreme Court crucial to the acceptability of a new democratic constitution, it insisted that a new Constitutional Court be established as the highest court in constitutional matters. The remaining ten members had not yet been appointed. Omar suggested that I discuss Cassese's invitation with Chaskalson, who encouraged me to consider the United Nations position. He considered it an important one, especially for a South African at that time. He thought too that, subject to the views of the government, it might be possible for me to accept the appointment to the Constitutional Court as well and take a leave of absence for a limited time. We discussed the precedent for such an appointment: Robert Jackson had been an associate justice of the United States Supreme Court when he accepted the appointment as the United States' chief prosecutor at the Nuremberg trial of Nazi criminals. Omar was happy with that solution, subject to the consent of Mandela.

At that point I received an impatient but polite call from Cassese, inquiring whether I had received his letter. I explained my position and said that I still needed to consult Mandela. He then informed me that if I was interested, I should let him know within thirty-six hours, because the issue was being taken up by President Clinton, Prime Minister Major, and President Yeltsin at the G7 meeting in Naples later that week. The Russian Federation had vetoed five of the previous eight nominees, and the question being raised was whether Russia was determined to wreck the tribunal or was objecting only to nominees from countries belonging to the North Atlantic Treaty Organization. I promised Cassese I would let him know as soon as possible. The attitude of Mandela was that if Omar and Chaskalson were satisfied with a two-year leave of absence, he was keen on my accepting what was the first important appointment by the international community of a South African since the Mandela government had assumed office a little more than two months earlier. In those circumstances I accepted, informing Judge Cassese two days after his initial inquiry. He was extremely relieved and indicated that he would inform Boutros-Ghali.

Soon after midnight I was awakened by a telephone call from a senior member of the Office of Legal Affairs of the United Nations—a call that would be my introduction to the bureaucratic idiosyncrasies of that organization. Apologizing for the lateness of the hour, he inquired whether I would be prepared to become chief prosecutor of the Yugoslavia tribunal. I had already indicated my acceptance earlier that day to Cassese, I said. He knew that, but Cassese was not authorized to offer the position on behalf of the secretary-general, and he was. Puzzled, I repeated what I had already told Cassese. The official stated that the vote in the Security Council on my nomination by the secretary-general would take place later that week.

Some months later I learned that the secretary-general had approached Mandela with the request that Mandela authorize him to inform the members of the Security Council informally that he, Mandela, supported my appointment. He agreed. Within a few days I was appointed by a unanimous vote of the Security Council. Then came my second introduction to the U.N.'s bureaucratic idiosyncrasies. Notwithstanding the formal appointment by the council, my assumption of office was dependent on a health clearance from a physician in South Africa who was on a United Nations panel of medical practitioners. Happily, that proved to be no more than a temporary delay.

What follows are some of my experiences in a new and unexpected period of my career, my years with the Goldstone Commission and the United Nations Criminal Tribunals for the former Yugoslavia and Rwanda.

The Goldstone Commission on
Public Violence and Intimidation

At the beginning of October 1991, Noleen and I moved into a new apartment near Cape Town's beautiful Waterfront. It commands a magnificent view over the Atlantic coast, including Robben Island, where Nelson Mandela and a number of his political colleagues were imprisoned for so many years. In 1991 that daily view of the island was a constant and joyful reminder that those days were forever behind us and that the negotiations intended to hand power to a democratically elected government were under way.

Less than two weeks after we moved, I received the telephone call that was to change our lives. It was from Kobie Coetsee, the minister of justice. He informed me of my selection as the chairperson of the Standing Commission of Inquiry Regarding the Prevention of Public Violence and Intimidation. During the preceding few weeks, there had been much press speculation as to who would be invited to hold that position. My name, among others, had been mentioned, and the call, therefore, did not come as a complete surprise. Nevertheless, the position was a daunting one, and I informed the minister that I needed time to consider my response. He agreed but added that it had taken more than two months for the parties to reach a consensus on the chairperson and four members of the commission. He pointed out that if I declined, the process would have to begin again, resulting in an inevitable delay that would be prejudicial to the peace process.

After due consideration and discussion with Noleen, I decided I would agree, subject to three conditions: (1) Because we had just moved from our home in Johannesburg to Cape Town, the commission would have to have an office in Cape Town; (2) Johan du Toit (J. J.) would be appointed as my assistant; and (3) I would be allowed to continue my work on the Supreme Court of Appeal, South Africa's final court of appeal, in Bloemfontein, and I would receive no remuneration additional to my judicial salary (this, it seemed to me, would be the best way of ensuring my public and private independence. In other words, my work on the commission would be volunteer).

On the following morning I flew to Pretoria to discuss these conditions with Coetsee. He unhesitatingly agreed to my terms and requested that I accompany him later that day to inform President de Klerk of my acceptance. The meeting was short. De Klerk thanked me for having agreed to take the position and expressed confidence that the violence then tearing at the fabric of South Africa and endangering the negotiation process would be of short duration. How wrong he turned out to be!

The four other members of the commission were Niel Rossouw, then attorney general of the Cape Province; Solly Sithole, a member of the Pretoria Bar; Lillian Baqwa, an attorney from Natal; and Gert Steyn, a recently retired president of a regional court. I had previously met Rossouw and Sithole, though very briefly, and did not know the other two members at all.

The first meeting of the commission was held in Pretoria on 26 October 1991, my fifty-third birthday. I was immediately impressed with the constructive and impartial attitude of my co-commissioners. It was agreed that Rossouw would resign as attorney general because that position would place his independence of the government in question and his decisions on prosecutions could create conflicts of interest. He and Gert Steyn, who would retain civil-service salaries, would serve as commissioners full-time, while the other members would serve on a part-time basis. During the life of the commission we met frequently, both formally and informally. I was fortunate in having been able to consult with my fellow commissioners on literally every decision we took, important or not. I cannot recall a single instance in which we did not agree on the chosen course of action.

Shortly before our first meeting, there had been serious political violence in the black township of Tembisa, near Johannesburg. We decided that that incident would be the subject of our first formal inquiry. I was immediately impressed with Sithole's confidence and good commonsense approach to the issues before us. He also displayed a strong personality and a fine sense of humor. I therefore asked him to head a subcommittee of the commission to conduct the inquiry. (Under the statute governing the commission, its powers could be delegated to a committee with a commissioner as the chairperson.) Sithole informed me, however, that he felt unqualified for the challenge. He said that as a black lawyer he felt a huge additional burden and responsibility and asked that I find someone else. He added that if he "made a mess" of the inquiry, it would be not only a personal calamity for him but also a setback for all black lawyers in South Africa. I replied that at that time in the transformation process, the credibility of the commission was crucial for its success. It was essential to demonstrate to the people of South Africa that this commission was different from preceding ones, all of which had been presided over by white male judges. It was essential that we conduct the affairs of this new commission, to the extent possible, in a nonracist, nonsexist, and impartial fashion. I then again appealed to Sithole to accept the position, and with much reluctance he agreed. Lillian Baqwa requested that she be a member of the committee. As the third member of the committee I appointed Bob Tucker, a leading lawyer and banker. Sithole presided over a very lengthy and difficult inquiry and acquitted himself with distinction. Today Sithole has a senior practice at the Pretoria Bar and has served a number of terms on the High Court Bench as an acting judge.

The commission's head office was in Pretoria. After some months we moved to Sandton, a satellite municipality of Johannesburg. Soon after the commission opened its doors, reports on violence began to pour in. The reports came from the police, from nongovernmental organizations, from political parties, and from the public. The most difficult issue we faced was the allocation of priorities, in that we simply did not have the resources to investigate every report. We decided to concentrate on the larger issues and, especially, the role of security forces and political parties in the violence. With regard to the latter, much ill will had grown up between the ANC and the Inkatha Freedom Party (IFP). Assassinations and attacks on innocent civilians had become the order of the day.

In my endeavor to establish wide credibility for the commission, I decided to hold meetings with the major political leaders, a move facilitated by certain foreign diplomats then serving in South Africa, in particular, those from Canada and Denmark. During the most repressive years of apartheid, foreign diplomats felt unusually free to intercede in South African affairs. Their homes became the focal point of meetings between political opponents who would not otherwise have met, especially across the color line. A good example was the initiative of a senior Canadian diplomatic husband and wife team, John and Elena Shram. Soon after my appointment, they decided that I should meet the spokesperson of the ANC, Gill Marcus, who had recently returned to South Africa after many years in exile. From the time of our first meeting in the Shram home, Gill and I became good friends, and she played an important role in facilitating meetings for me with the ANC leadership. In the first democratic Parliament elected in April 1994, she was appointed chairperson of the Finance Committee of the House of Assembly. Mandela later appointed her deputy minister of finance. She is now a deputy governor of the South African Reserve Bank.

In 1992, the commission published an interim report listing, in historical sequence, the causes of the violence. It included the three-hundred-year history of racial oppression in South Africa; the enforcement by the police of the hated apartheid laws in the years after 1948; the disparity in wealth in the country; and the rivalry between the ANC and IFP. According to the statute that governed the commission, reports were required to be presented to the president, who then made discretionary decisions as to whether and when the reports were to be made public. In keeping with past practice, de Klerk withheld our reports until relevant government departments had been given the opportunity of studying and reporting to him on the contents. More important, when reports were released, they were always accompanied by a government press release with its own spin. In the case of this interim report, the government's press communiqué suggested, quite erroneously, that the commission had ascribed the causes of violence in South Africa to the activities of the African National Congress and the Inkatha Freedom Party. And that is how the evening newspapers reported the findings. Reporters had little time to read what was a fairly lengthy report and had to rely on the government's slanted version.

The evening the interim report was released, Mandela returned from a trip abroad. The next morning he addressed an important ANC meeting. He castigated the commission and accused it of bias and incompetence. I felt deep hurt and frustration, because it was obvious to me that Mandela had based his remarks on the newspaper reports and that he, too, had not read the actual report.

Early that afternoon I received a telephone call from Mandela. (In his usual fashion he made the call himself.) He immediately apologized to me for the unfair remarks he had made, which indeed had been based on the news reports. Only after his address had he been able to read the report itself. He had found it to be objective and fair and agreed with most of what it contained. The second reason for his call was to inform me that he had called a press conference which was to take place a couple of hours later. He requested that I consent to his telling the conference that he had apologized to me, and that I had accepted his apology. Needless to say, I was most relieved and readily agreed to his request. In my experience, few leaders would have acted in that fashion. To apologize was one thing, to call a press conference to correct the record was another. This was one of many incidents then and later that demonstrated the innate fairness and sense of justice of the man whose opponents had imprisoned him for a third of his life.

This incident left me in no doubt that if the commission was to retain its credibility, de Klerk's practice of holding back the release of our reports had to end. The following day I released a media statement stating my concern and called upon the president to release our reports immediately upon their submission to him. De Klerk's response came swiftly. He would undertake to release all of the commission's reports within twenty-four hours of receiving them. He faithfully carried out that undertaking.

A few weeks after the commission had been appointed, I was contacted by the French ambassador, Joëlle Bourgois. She invited me to lunch at her beautiful Cape Town home. The purpose of the meeting, she told me, was to inquire whether her government could be helpful to my commission. The area that immediately sprang to mind was policing. I informed her that I would be interested in learning about policing practices in France and especially the approach to mass demonstrations and marches. I added, much to her amusement, that I was particularly interested in policing in the wine areas! A few months later I spent ten fascinating days with the French police, who shared much with me. I was interested to learn that since the time of the French Revolution, France had had two distinct forces, the Police Nationale, under the Ministry of the Interior, and the Gendarmerie, under the Ministry of Defense. Each force has the same number of members, and they keep a close watch on each other. The remark about policing in the wine regions had a most enjoyable sequel—a memorable weekend as guests of Moët and Chandon at its luxurious mansion in Champagne.

During June 1992, while I was in France, the terrible massacre of innocent people in the black township of Boipatong, near Johannesburg, took place. The ANC accused the IFP of having organized it. Needless to say, the IFP immediately denied any involvement. That incident brought the peace process to a stop, and it was many months before it was resumed. It was obvious that the commission would urgently have to inquire into the massacre and that I would have to return home for that purpose. The day after the incident I received a call from the minister of justice, who told me that de Klerk had requested that I appoint a leading international jurist to sit with me in the inquiry. I readily agreed to do so. At that time it was most unusual for the South African government to consider any foreign involvement in the affairs of our country, so I welcomed this opportunity.

That evening we had been invited for dinner to the home of Roger Arrera, a judge and human rights activist. While dressing for dinner, I discussed possible international jurists with Noleen. My first choice was former Chief Justice Proful Bhagwati of India, whom I had met a few months earlier in Johannesburg when he was attending an international conference on bills of rights. Over drinks with the Arreras, I talked about the request from de Klerk. Arrera asked me whom I had in mind, and I said my first choice was Bhagwati. He looked pleasantly surprised and said that if I had asked for his advice he would have made the same suggestion. I asked if he could obtain Bhagwati's telephone number. That was no problem, he assured me. Within minutes I had Bhagwati's home number in New Delhi.

The next morning I was able to contact Bhagwati, who was in Bombay. I explained my request to him. It was a Friday morning, and Bhagwati asked me when I intended to begin the inquiry. I informed him that I was flying to Johannesburg from London on the following Wednesday evening and that the inquiry would begin the next day. Then and there Bhagwati undertook plans to meet me in London and travel to South Africa on the same flight. That was just the beginning of his unusual generosity with his time and involvement. We sat together for many weeks in three sessions of a difficult and complex inquiry.

While in London, I also requested a leading expert on policing, Professor P.A.J. ("Tank") Waddington, director of Criminal Justice Studies at the University of Reading, to help the commission investigate emerging allegations of police complicity in the Boipatong massacre. He agreed and suggested that I arrange for two experienced British police officers to assist him. The British government, and especially the junior minister at the Foreign Office, Baroness Linda Chalker, were extremely helpful. The night before the inquiry was to begin, Bhagwati, Waddington, and two seasoned police officers joined me on the flight back to Johannesburg. Waddington's investigation brought to light the inefficiency of the South African Police in the incident. However, he found no evidence of police complicity in the massacre.

The growing support of South Africans for the work of the commission and the increasing attention it was attracting abroad made us bolder. In the second half of 1992 I informed de Klerk that we needed our own investigation teams. Until then, we had been obliged to rely on the South African Police—an arrangement that was obviously unsatisfactory. The police had little if any credibility among the majority of South Africans and were perceived, often with justification, as being opposed to the transformation of our society. Reluctantly, the government agreed. It was clear that the investigators who were to make up our teams would have to be members of the South African Police—there was no other South African organization to draw from. As a consequence, I cautioned the government that the public should be assured these special investigators were suitable for work with an independent commission. I suggested three steps to attain that goal. The first was to publish in the national press the names of the fifteen members of the South African Police who would comprise the teams and to invite the public to inform the commission of any information relating to their unsuitability for the task. The second was to request senior foreign police officers to work with the South Africans. And the third was to have independent attorneys join each of the five teams to be stationed in the main urban centers.

The government balked at all three proposals, in particular the one relating to foreign police officers working in South Africa. At that time the government was still in its apartheid mode of resenting any role by the international community in the internal affairs of the country. I nonetheless persisted, and eventually the government agreed to all three. The names of the police officers were published in due course, with objections presented to only one of them. The grievances appeared to be justified, and the person in question was not appointed.

I personally requested that the Commissioner of Police appoint one police officer, Major Frank Dutton. A year earlier, Dutton had achieved prominence by publicizing information on an operation in which a senior police officer had ordered an attack on, and the murder of, supporters of the ANC. The officer, however, had inadvertently given an incorrect address to the assassins. As a result, those killed were supporters of the IFP. In acting as he did, Dutton displayed unusual courage. He is a man without strong political feelings but with a deep belief in the need for complete integrity in police investigations, regardless of the consequences. He was the ideal police officer to work with the commission, and over the following months, he would play a key role in the commission's most sensitive investigations. The suggestion that Dutton would be an asset came from Jacob Zuma, the chairperson of the ANC in KwaZulu Natal who would later become the deputy president of South Africa. I had good reason to be grateful to Zuma for his recommendation of Dutton. After I became the chief prosecutor of the Yugoslavia tribunal, Dutton approached me for a position with the investigation section of the Office of the Prosecutor. I was delighted at the prospect of having him on board, and he successfully applied for a United Nations post. For some time he was the senior official in the prosecutor's office in Sarajevo. More recently, Dutton has returned to South Africa to head a new, special rapid-reaction police unit.

I approached the Law Society of South Africa for assistance in identifying appropriate senior attorneys who would be prepared to serve with the units. The society responded positively to this request, and within a few days we had an attorney for each of the five units. They were senior members of the profession and participated fully in important and sensitive decisions.

At the time of these negotiations, Douglas Hurd, the British foreign minister, led a European Union delegation to South Africa. He was joined by the foreign ministers of Portugal and Denmark (the "troika"). When I met with them, I reported on the proposed investigation teams and the need for foreign police officers. They agreed that the European Union members could supply suitably qualified police officers for the work. Within weeks we had the first of a series of recruits from the United Kingdom, Denmark, Portugal, France, and the Netherlands.

They played a crucial role in making the work of the investigation units credible, efficient, and effective.

At the same meeting, Hurd inquired whether the European Union might contribute in other areas. When I informed him that we required financial assistance for witness protection, he asked how much I had in mind. Without any prior consideration, I suggested one hundred thousand rands, the equivalent then of approximately twenty thousand dollars. Hurd asked one of the Brussels bureaucrats in his party whether there would be any difficulty in contributing that amount. The man replied that he would have to consider the request and consult on the matter when he returned to Brussels. The Danish foreign minister, Uffe Elleman-Jensen, with a naughty gleam in his eye, intervened and said that he would hate to give the bureaucrats any trouble and that Denmark would make the contribution.

Not long after that meeting, the Danish government invited me to Copenhagen to meet with government officials and the commissioner of police to explain the work of the commission. The Norwegian government also extended an invitation to visit Oslo. These trips helped pave the way for subsequent assistance from those two countries. During my stay in Oslo, I was contacted by Abdul Minty, a long-time member of the ANC who had successfully led the movement to have a universal arms embargo enforced against South Africa and who in recent years had been living in exile. Minty and I met for breakfast and soon found much in common.

On a two-day vacation, Noleen and I traveled through the fjords to Bergen, where I had requested an inexpensive hotel room. When we were shown rather large executive accommodations, I wondered if there had been some mistake. In the room we found a beautiful arrangement of flowers and a card from Minty wishing us a pleasant stay. I called him to thank him for his kindness, and he inquired whether the room was to our liking. My concern over the financial implications made him laugh. Minty said he had informed the manager that I was a very important visitor and should be treated accordingly. I shall return presently to my association with Minty.

Soon after the establishment of the investigation units, the commission decided to embark on a new inquiry—not into specific incidents of violence but into ways of preventing violence during public marches, demonstrations, and pickets. Such an investigation was not only urgent but of immediate and long-term relevance. Public demonstrations were the only peaceful means by which the disenfranchised majority in South Africa could make a powerful political statement. In times of uncertainty and political volatility, such protests obviously heightened the potential for violence and for confrontation between participants and police. Demonstrations were, by this time, taking place on a daily basis in cities, towns, and villages all over the country, though the demonstrators were refusing to seek permission from the police and local authorities, as required by law. In consequence, each march and protest was fraught with the potential for violence and injury. The authorities were unaware of the location of marches, their duration, or the number of participants. Similarly, the demonstrators or marchers did not know if the police would intervene and prevent what were illegal activities.

I had recently attended a seminar at the University of Natal on policing in the "new" South Africa. One of the participants was Professor Phillip Heymann, director of the Center for Criminal Justice at Harvard Law School. I discussed with him my concern about the potential for violence in light of the hundreds of public demonstrations that had become a feature of daily life in South Africa. I also told him that I was considering setting up a public inquiry into the matter. During our discussion, the idea of using an international panel of experts was conceived. An international perspective would help convince all sides that what we might expect of them was consistent with practices and procedures in other democracies. Heymann readily agreed to act as the convener and

chairperson of the multinational advisory panel of experts, which was
to include five South African and five foreign experts.

I anticipated that the government would again object to the use of foreign experts. Special funding was necessary for the project, and instead
of having to convince the government to provide it, I requested the governments of the participating countries to meet their individual costs.
The governments of the United Kingdom, the United States, Canada,
and the Netherlands agreed. I kept the minister of justice apprised on
an informal basis, and he fully supported my proposal. In May 1992 I
announced the appointment of the multinational advisory panel.

The inquiry into mass marches and demonstrations was held in Cape
Town over a period of two weeks. Competent reports were submitted,
in particular on behalf of the South African Police, the ANC, and the
IFP. As the inquiry was coming to an end, it became apparent that
the parties were not far apart. There was general agreement that each
side should be informed of what the other was intending to do; that
notice was to be given by the organizers of demonstrations, marches,
and pickets; and that permission for such gatherings should not un-
reasonably be withheld. The sticking point was that the predominantly
black parties were not prepared to act in accordance with laws passed
by a Parliament from which they were excluded. I approached the legal
representatives of the parties with the suggestion that I draft an agreement setting out the terms under which marches should be held during the period of transformation. They agreed. One stumbling block,
however, was the IFP's insistence that its followers be allowed to carry
traditional or "cultural" weapons in their marches. On no account was
the commission prepared to accept such a demand. In previous reports
it had issued strong recommendations against anyone being allowed to
carry any form of weapon in public.

The South African Police and the ANC signed the agreement, but
the IFP refused because of a provision to the effect that "participants

in demonstrations should not be in possession of dangerous weapons."
Unwilling to allow that irrational and unjustifiable objection to sink
the agreement, I decided to release the agreement with the public announcement that the IFP, while insisting on the right to carry their traditional weapons, had accepted all the other terms. The agreement recognized the right to demonstrate peacefully in public and the duty of
police to protect that right. That right had never been the law or the perception of the South African government and certainly not that of the
South African Police. The agreement went on to make provisions for
notice of demonstrations and for negotiations in order to resolve the
manner in which they were to be conducted. The details that organizers were to make available to the authorities were set out. I informed
the parties that I would make the agreement public on 16 July 1992.

The day before the announcement, while attending a law seminar
outside Johannesburg, I was called out of a session to take a call from
Kobie Coetsee. He said that the Cabinet had been informed that I intended to announce the agreement on public demonstrations and
marches the following day. I confirmed that that was so. He said that de
Klerk had requested me not to do so, however. I inquired as to his reason. Coetsee said that the effect of the agreement was that the commission was condoning public demonstrations in breach of the law of the
land. I replied that I was irrevocably committed to making the agreement public the following morning. Indeed I had already issued copies
to the media. Coetsee sounded unhappy, but there was little he could do
about the matter. An hour later I received another call from Coetsee; de
Klerk was now requesting that my announcement make it clear that the
commission did not intend to suggest that members of the public hold
demonstrations or marches in breach of the laws of the land. Again,
I told Coetsee that I could not do that, because I was not prepared to
suggest that black South Africans, none of whom were represented in
Parliament, should consider themselves obliged to follow those laws,

particularly at that time in our history. In reaction, the minister said he was surprised to hear such a view expressed by a member of the judiciary. We agreed that it would serve no purpose to pursue the matter in a telephone discussion, and we left it at that.

On the day the agreement was made public, the ANC had planned a mass march on the Union Buildings, the seat of government in Pretoria. They had given notice that the march would begin in the center of the city and that some ninety thousand people were expected to participate. The Pretoria municipality and the South African Police were concerned that the city would be completely dislocated. The ANC, however, had refused to negotiate a route or to reduce the number of marchers. An impasse had been reached, and it was feared that violence and injury would be the order of the day if the police interfered with the march.

On the morning of the announcement I received yet another call from the minister of justice. "I have phoned to confess that you were right and we were wrong," he said. From the moment the agreement was made public, he explained, the ANC organizers had pledged to negotiate with the police and the local authority with regard to the route of the march and a decrease in the number of marchers. I pointed out to Coetsee that when people are made part of a process and feel fully consulted, they generally adhere to the terms they agree upon. That is really what democratic government is all about. He did not disagree.

There was compliance with the agreement from that time until it was replaced by a new statute passed by the first democratic Parliament, after the April 1994 elections. That statute was in line with the agreement drafted by the commission and based upon the recommendations of the multinational advisory panel.

The deployment of our own investigation units proved to be a turning point for the commission. Crucial to our success was our ability to investigate matters relating to the security forces themselves (including complaints against the police) without having to work with the police authorities. Without our own investigators we would not have been able to make the first important breakthrough in investigating what was widely referred to as "third force" activities by the security forces. For some years there had been allegations implicating the police and the army in promoting the violence between the ANC and the IFP in an effort to sabotage the negotiations that would inevitably lead to black majority rule. Such an eventuality was anathema to many whites in government service. Also, there were continuing allegations that the security forces were sabotaging the liberation movements themselves.

Until about October 1992, the commission had found no credible evidence to establish the existence of the alleged third force. Then there was a dramatic breakthrough. Joao Cuna, a twenty-nine-year-old Mozambican, went to a liberal Afrikaans newspaper called *Die Vryeweekblad* and asked for assistance. He claimed to be under the control of white men who had forced him to participate in attacking homes belonging to ANC activists. He said that he had helped launch an attack from a hotel in the Pietermaritzburg area of KwaZulu Natal. On the way to the attack, he claimed that the people with him had shot bystanders at a taxi stand. That night, after an attack in which a number of people were killed, they had slept at the hotel. The following morning Cuna was paid four thousand rands. He was being pressed to continue with these activities against his will—and he feared for his life.

Cuna's allegations came at a time when attacks of the kind he described were all too common, especially in KwaZulu Natal. A number of his versions, however, were contradictory. After his story was published in the newspaper, it was decided that his allegations should be investigated by the commission's Natal investigation team, headed at that time by Frank Dutton.

I asked Colonel Henk Heslinga to assist in the investigation. Heslinga, who worked at our head office in Pretoria, was the most senior member of the South African Police serving with the commission. He had been seconded by the police to assist the commission from the day it began its work. When I first met Heslinga, he volunteered that he had previously been a member of Koevoet, a notorious unit that had operated against the South West Africa People's Organization (SWAPO), the most important liberation army fighting for the independence of Namibia. If that disqualified him from serving with the commission, he would understand and arrange to be replaced. I was impressed with Heslinga's candor and told him that he should remain. He gave me no reason to regret that decision. After the investigation units were set up, I decided that Heslinga should continue to work from the head office of the commission and not be involved directly with the units. Toward the end of the commission's life, when we were investigating serious criminal conduct on the part of the most senior members of the South African Police, Heslinga felt that he had a conflict of interests and asked that I agree to his leaving the commission and returning to regular police work. I had no option but to agree. Today Heslinga occupies a senior position in the reorganized South African Police Service.

To return to Cuna. Heslinga astutely took Cuna from hotel to hotel in the Pietermaritzburg area, and he eventually pointed out the one in question. In the hope that the hotel bill had been paid with a credit card, Heslinga asked the manager of the hotel for access to the credit card slips for the period when Cuna alleged that he had slept at the hotel. A Diners Club slip he found recorded payment for three rooms on the night in question. It was in the name of Africa Risk Analysis Consultants (ARAC).

To ascertain details about ARAC, it was necessary to obtain information from the head office of Diners Club. Their management had informed Heslinga that they were not prepared to divulge any information about their customers. I decided that this was an appropriate case in which to implement the powers of search and seizure given to me by the commission's statute. The firm of attorneys where I had served articles of clerkship many years before acted for Diners Club. I contacted a partner, who handled the account, and informed him that I needed the information in question but that I preferred to obtain the information informally rather than send in investigators who would have to seize the records. Within minutes I received a call from the managing director of Diners Club, who informed me that a warrant should be faxed to him. Thereafter he would immediately give our investigators the information required. He added that ARAC was their largest customer and that he hoped we would not close them down. Over forty cards were listed in the names of ARAC employees, and millions of rands were spent annually on transport and hotel expenses. I knew at that moment that we were onto something big.

The offices of ARAC were in a large building in a shopping complex in a suburb of Pretoria. Cuna could provide only one name of those he alleged were in control of his murderous attacks — Ferdi Barnard, a notorious former member of the South African Police who had been imprisoned for three murders and had recently been released after serving his sentence. He stood trial for a number of other murders, including that of a well-respected academic, Dr. David Webster. After much discussion, the commission decided to launch a search of the premises of ARAC. From a visual inspection it occupied considerable office space and, by virtue of the funds available to it, we had little doubt that it was a government-controlled operation.

I requested that Torie Pretorius, a colleague of J. J. du Toit in the attorney general's office, lead the raid. Pretorius is a very competent lawyer and an excellent investigator. After the commission's term of office ended, Pretorius continued to investigate serious criminal conduct by government agents during apartheid times. He is now a senior member of the office of the director of National Prosecutions.

Pretorius was accompanied by Heslinga and members of the Johannesburg Investigation Unit. Having decided that they should be joined by regular uniformed and armed police, I contacted the headquarters of the South African Police in Pretoria and explained that one of the commission's units was going on a dangerous mission and would require special protection. I need hardly add that I provided no details of the mission. The backup force was speedily provided and about fifteen uniformed and armed police officers accompanied Pretorius and the investigators.

When the group arrived at the offices of ARAC, Pretorius produced the search warrant I had signed and demanded access to files relating to Ferdi Barnard. The employees, faced with a determined group backed up by a contingent of uniformed police, immediately complied. Pretorius called me from the offices and informed me that ARAC was a front for a large office of military intelligence called (quaintly) the Directorate of Covert Collection (DCC). I instructed him to continue the search for the Barnard files and no others. I realized that if I had ordered a general search, it would have led to an urgent court proceeding and that we would have had little prospect of justifying a fishing expedition. I immediately called the minister of justice, however, and informed him that officials of the commission were at that moment raiding a department of military intelligence. Coetsee's response was, "Judge, you must do what you have to do."

Pretorius took a number of files, one of which related to an operation code-named "Operation Baboon," whose main purpose was to gather information with which to blackmail senior members of the ANC and other opponents of apartheid. Other shocking details appeared from the files, including the running of a brothel in order to photograph important people in compromising situations. I found it morally unacceptable that a man of Barnard's past and reputation should have been employed by military intelligence in any capacity at all.

When I received the documents in question, the difficult question was how to handle them. Under the commission's statute, a report on all *inquiries* conducted was to be given to the president. I had little doubt that, notwithstanding de Klerk's earlier efforts to release our reports promptly, a report of this nature would not have been made public by the government without the fullest internal inquiry. I was also certain that a cover-up had begun within minutes of the raid. After due consideration and discussion with my co-commissioners, I formed the view that the term *inquiries,* as properly interpreted in the statute, related to formal inquiries held by the commission or committees of the commission in which evidence was solicited from witnesses. Any information obtained through search and seizure was a different matter, and, indeed, the commission was under no statutory obligation to report on it at all. We decided that with regard to the nature of the evidence, it was important to make the information public as soon as possible. I called a press conference in Johannesburg for the following Monday afternoon.

This was only the second press conference I had called since the beginning of the commission. (My customary form of communication was a written release.) The conference was well attended by the local and international press, and I was accompanied by three members of the commission. The disclosures could not have come at a worse time for de Klerk. On that day he was returning from an international rugby game he had attended in London with the British prime minister, John Major. At Heathrow Airport, in answer to a question from a journalist, he stated that he was satisfied that the South African security forces were not involved with third-force activities. The commission's disclosures proved his statement to be incorrect. The details I furnished at the press conference received wide publicity in South Africa and abroad and confirmed what had, for many months, been alleged by the ANC and a number of investigative journalists.

At the conclusion of the press conference I noticed Abdul Minty in the audience. As I moved to greet him, he signaled his discomfort and he waved me away. I whispered my hotel room number, and a little later he joined me there. He explained that he did not think it advisable for me to be seen speaking to him at that time because of his activities, which the South African security establishment considered treasonous. My next meeting with Minty was in more auspicious circumstances, the inauguration of President Mandela. Before the ceremony began, I noticed him some distance away in the company of Kenneth Kaunda, the former president of Zambia, and Archbishop Trevor Huddleston, an English Episcopalian priest who for many years had courageously fought apartheid. I went to greet Minty. We spontaneously hugged each other, and I whispered in his ear, "Eighteen months ago we were unable to greet each other in public and today we are embracing in front of thousands of people!" This incident demonstrated how fundamental and rapid our change had been. Minty was later appointed as deputy director-general of the Department of Foreign Affairs in Pretoria.

When President de Klerk returned to South Africa, he requested an urgent meeting with me, at which he made no effort to hide his resentment of my having made the information public. Opposition political parties were demanding that the commission be given authority to hold the widest inquiry into military intelligence, though the government was not prepared even to consider such a demand. The conservative press, not unexpectedly, castigated the commission for its unpatriotic actions. Eventually de Klerk appointed the head of the South African Air Force, General Pierre Steyn, to investigate the allegations made by the commission. It was agreed that Torie Pretorius, representing the commission, would work with General Steyn. A few weeks later de Klerk, to the surprise of most South Africans, suddenly announced the dismissal of twenty-three members of the South African Defense Force, including generals and brigadiers. That action, he stated, was taken as a result of information given to him by Steyn.

The raid on military intelligence and President de Klerk's actions in response had an unexpected and beneficial outcome. It laid to rest a myth harbored by the security forces that they were impregnable. It also opened the way for members of those forces to consider divulging information to the commission.

On the evening of Saturday, 10 April 1993, I was scheduled to leave for a visit to New York. One of the reasons was to brief the Security Council of the United Nations on violence in South Africa and the work of the commission. That morning I received a frantic call from Barbara Masekela, then Mandela's personal assistant (who later became South Africa's ambassador to France). She informed me that Chris Hani, chairperson of the South African Communist Party, and one of the country's most popular leaders, had been shot, though she did not know whether he had been killed. Soon after, an announcement was made that Hani had died of bullet wounds to the head. His assassin was a young Polish immigrant, Janus Waluz, who had been persuaded to assassinate Hani by Clive Derby-Lewis, a member of the right-wing Conservative Party. Derby-Lewis was the husband of Gaye Derby-Lewis, who, after my Govender opinion of 1982, had complained to President Botha that his government was not taking steps to eject blacks who were moving into white areas. Both Gaye and Clive Derby-Lewis and Janus Waluz stood trial for the murder. Mrs. Derby-Lewis was acquitted, but her husband and Waluz were convicted and sentenced to life imprisonment. Both applied for amnesty from the Truth and Reconciliation Commission. They were unsuccessful.

I was faced with the dilemma of whether to cancel the New York trip in order to conduct an inquiry into the assassination. After reflection, I decided to leave for New York, meet with the Security Council, and return as soon as possible. The assassination brought South Africa closer to a bloodbath than any other event since the start of the negotiation process in 1990. Fortunately, de Klerk took the unusual step of order-ing that the national television station be made available to Mandela to enable him to make calls for peace and nonviolence. It worked, and the reactionary violence was kept at a low level.

Soon after I arrived in New York, I received the news that Waluz had been arrested, together with Clive and Gaye Derby-Lewis. A police ex-amination of Gaye Derby-Lewis's computer resulted in a printout of a death list. Hani's name topped the list; mine was fifth. I believe that the reason for the inclusion of my name was Mrs. Derby-Lewis's resent-ment of the Govender opinion and its consequences. Before my return, I was informed by the commissioner of police that the government had decided that I would have round-the-clock police protection. That pro-tection continued until the middle of 1998.

Living with bodyguards has slight advantages and serious disadvan-tages. The former include having the convenience of being driven wher-ever one has to go without the hassle of looking for parking and the ability to read the newspaper in the car. And, of course, not being con-cerned about the amount of alcohol one drinks at a dinner party. The greatest disadvantage is the invasion of one's liberty and privacy that comes with it. I especially felt that when I was at home in Cape Town. On a lovely summer's evening, I frequently yearned to go for a walk along the beach front and was not prepared to inconvenience my body-guards by calling them out at short notice. What makes the system bear-able at all is the concern, sensitivity, and kindness of the many body-guards we have had both in South Africa and the Netherlands.

The meetings I held at the United Nations were, at the time, an un-usual experience for a South African. Jim Steward was South Africa's permanent representative at the United Nations. He looked after me most attentively and accompanied me to a meeting with that month's Security Council president, Ambassador Jansheed Marker of Pakistan. Marker could not have been more supportive or friendly. He explained the procedure that is followed when the Security Council meets informally with a visitor. The president does not preside, and one of the other members acts as chairperson. After chatting with me for about thirty minutes, Marker took me into the meeting, where I was warmly greeted by Madeleine Albright, then the permanent representative of the United States, and Sir David Hannay, her British counterpart. The members were most interested in the work of the commission and expressed full support for it.

Later the same day, at the invitation of its chairperson, Ambassador Ibrahim Gambari of Nigeria, I attended a special meeting of the United Nations Special Committee on Apartheid. Again, with one exception, the reception was extremely warm. Immediately after my address, the leader of the Pan Africanist Congress mission in New York launched an attack on the commission and on me personally. I really did not know what the appropriate response should be. Before I could react, the deputy leader of the ANC at the United Nations, Kingsley Makhubela, came to my rescue. After his response, there was nothing I needed to add. I was moved at the manner in which I was welcomed as a fellow African. I experienced for the first time the realization that skin color does not define who is an African, regardless of one's country of origin. This was confirmed many times over when, from 1994 to 1996, as the chief prosecutor of the Rwanda War Crimes Tribunal, I visited a number of African countries.

While in New York, I had an appointment to meet with Dr. Franklin Thomas, then president of the Ford Foundation. Within minutes of my arriving in his office I received calls from de Klerk and Mandela, both requesting that the commission hold a formal investigation into the Hani assassination. I shall never forget how warmly and spontaneously Franklin Thomas gave his office over to me and put his secretary, telephone, and fax machine at my disposal. From there the necessary instructions were issued for the preliminary public inquiry to be held in

Johannesburg a few days later. In light of the advanced police investigations, the Hani inquiry focused on the acts and areas of violence that erupted in the days following that tragic event.

As South Africa's first democratic election was approaching, so too was the fear that right-wing elements in the country would attempt to disrupt it. The inquiry into mass demonstrations had been so successful that the commission decided to repeat the exercise and investigate ways of reducing the potential for violence in that election. Again, a multinational panel of experts was assembled. They came from Zimbabwe, Canada, Denmark, the United States, and Ghana. Phillip Heymann again agreed to head the panel. A few months before the work was due to begin, however, he called to inform me that President Clinton had nominated him to be deputy attorney general of the United States. He expressed his apology for having to let me down, and I responded that I would release him from his undertaking only if he found a suitable substitute. A few weeks later we met in Washington, D.C., and he suggested Charles Ruff, a leading attorney there, as his replacement. Heymann and I met with Ruff in his office and discussed the matter. Ruff was immediately interested but asked for a few days to consider the offer and discuss it with his wife, Sue, and his law partners. During that week I had a private meeting with Senator Paul Simon, who was particularly interested in the work of my commission. In the course of briefing him, I told him of my offer to Chuck Ruff, whose decision I awaited. Senator Simon was then a member of the Senate Judiciary Committee, which had not yet confirmed Phillip Heymann's appointment. To his amusement, I asked the senator whether, in the event that Ruff chose not to replace Heymann, he would grant me standing before his committee so that I could oppose the confirmation of Heymann as deputy attorney general. After all, I had a prior commitment from him! Senator Simon immediately agreed. In any event, Ruff agreed, and we had an ideal replacement for Heymann. (In 1997 Ruff became President Clinton's legal adviser and was faced with the complicated legal problems that arose during the most difficult period of the president's terms of office. It was Ruff who was given the unenviable task of making the closing statement for the president in the impeachment proceedings before the Judiciary Committee of the House of Representatives.)

The inquiry into election violence produced a report that many countries have found useful. Three of the foreign panel members were later appointed as members of South Africa's Independent Electoral Commission, which had the incredibly complex task of organizing South Africa's first democratic election.

The last inquiry of the commission was probably its most important and most dramatic. It came about as a result of a fallout between two rogues—both members of the now notorious Vlakplaas Unit of the South African Security Police. That unit was involved, during apartheid times and during the transition to democracy, with political murders, massive frauds, gunrunning, and other criminal activity. Chappies Klopper, whose life had been threatened by his superior officer, decided to disclose the nefarious activities of Vlakplaas. Concerned that the commission would not do anything about his allegations, he initially approached Peter Hansen, a senior diplomat in the Danish embassy in Pretoria. Hansen approached me for advice, and I suggested that he persuade Klopper to speak to me. Unbeknownst to me until over a year later, the Danish embassy arranged for a considerable payment to Klopper in return for his agreement to see me. Some years later Klopper stated during the criminal trial of the notorious former head of Vlakplaas, Eugene de Kock, that the commission had paid him. It was hardly relevant at that stage, and the true source of the payment did not emerge.

My first meeting with Klopper was in the darkened swimming pool area of the hotel in which I was living in Sandton. He revealed little more than that his former commanding officer, Eugene de Kock, was still involved in criminal third-force activities involving political violence. That came as a surprise, because about a year earlier de Kock and a number of his colleagues in Vlakplaas had retired from the South African Police and had received handsome cash payments from the government. The reason given for their retirement and the payments was that the ANC had blackened their names to the extent that they could no longer play any relevant role as police. Klopper informed me that de Kock was still using seven passports issued to him under false names, which he disclosed to me. He promised more information at future meetings.

I decided that the most efficient manner of checking on the veracity of Klopper's information was to search the files of the Department of Home Affairs in order to find the files kept under de Kock's false names. I armed Major Dutton with the necessary search warrant, which he presented at the relevant office in Pretoria. Indeed there were files on the names in question. They were all empty, however, save for a note to the effect that any inquiries were to be referred to Lieutenant-General Johan le Roux, a senior police officer at the police headquarters in Pretoria. I had no doubt that the officials at the Home Affairs Department had already alerted le Roux, and I instructed Dutton to approach him for information. Le Roux was not forthcoming and could not offer an explanation as to why de Kock should have been in possession of false passports.

On the following day I had another meeting with Klopper. He told me that he was one of six members of Vlakplaas who on the previous afternoon had been called into le Roux's office. There they were informed that the Goldstone Commission was getting involved in sensitive matters concerning the unit. The members were instructed by le Roux, so Klopper said, to leave no stone unturned in an effort to find evidence with which to blackmail me. Two of them were dispatched to the office of the income tax commissioner in Johannesburg in order to obtain my tax files for the preceding twenty years in an attempt to find some nondisclosure of income on my part. Two others were instructed to take steps to inquire whether I was conducting an extramarital affair.

The reaction of le Roux was the best corroboration of the information given me by Klopper. In the following days Klopper added considerably to the information. He implicated three senior police officers in serious criminal activities. One of them was le Roux. The other two were the deputy commissioner of police, General Basie Smit, and one of his senior colleagues, General Krappies Engelbrecht. The commission's lawyers and investigation team worked full-time on this matter.

When sufficient corroboration had been obtained, I decided to request additional assistance from President de Klerk. I met him alone at his official residence in Cape Town. He was visibly shocked at what I told him. I asked him to order the National Intelligence Agency (the South African equivalent of the Central Intelligence Agency) to assist me in the investigation. I also requested unlimited funds for witness protection. He immediately agreed and gave the necessary instructions to relevant officials. The spontaneity of his reaction convinced me that he had no knowledge of the allegations of complicity in the violence of the most senior police officials.

The details of the investigation were made public in a dramatic joint press conference that de Klerk and I held in Pretoria about six weeks before the April 1994 election. De Klerk's suspension of the three police generals was announced at that conference. The three generals and the commissioner of police, General Johan van der Merwe, issued angry denials.

The effect of the earlier raid on the DCC and the dismissal of the senior military officers had already made many in the security establishment nervous about the operation of the commission. The more evidence we collected, the more concerned many senior police officers became. I must confess that notwithstanding the criminality already uncovered, I was still shocked by some of the revelations coming to light. We uncovered convincing evidence that the security police had bombed Khotso House, an office building in the center of Johannesburg. The offices of the South African Council of Churches (SACC), which for years had fought apartheid, were situated in that building. So, too, were the offices of the Black Sash, an organization of courageous women who engaged in public protests against apartheid. In his application for amnesty to the Truth and Reconciliation Commission, General van der Merwe, who had consistently objected to the inquiry and so vociferously denied his involvement and that of his associates, confessed to his part in ordering the bombing of the building. The evidence we collected also disclosed that the then minister of law and order, Adriaan Vlok, attended a function at Vlakplaas where he toasted the police officers responsible for the bombing. Later,Vlok disclosed his involvement in this incident in his own amnesty application.

These activities by the commission gave rise to additional threats against my life and eventually against Noleen's as well. And, as might be expected, a number of our witnesses were threatened. The British and Danish governments were especially generous in the assistance they offered in this area. Peter Hansen and the Danish ambassador, Peter Bruckner, persuaded their government to accept a significant number of the commission's witnesses and their families under a witness-protection program. Another important witness was sent to England. Some months later, when this activity became public in Denmark, the Danish minister of justice requested that I join him at a press conference in Copenhagen to explain to the Danish public the importance of the program.

In January 1994 Noleen and I arranged to visit our witnesses in Den-

mark and England. Two days prior to our departure I received a disturb-
ing telephone call at our Sandton hotel. The caller refused to tell me his
name, but he knew in detail what investigations were under way and
what my movements had been the previous day and what I had planned
for that day. He warned me that Noleen and I were in imminent danger of being killed and that we should leave the hotel without delay.
I immediately contacted a senior official of the National Intelligence
Agency and was told to take the threat seriously. I was advised to move
forward by two days our departure for London. I was also told that we
should spend the remainder of the day in the Sandton Shopping Center and to leave from there for the Johannesburg International Airport.
On no account were we to go to our room and pack our bags. Arrangements were made for an armed guard to accompany us on the flight to
London. The British ambassador, Sir Anthony Reeve, undertook to have
us met at Heathrow Airport and to arrange accommodations for us in
London.

Under the protection of our bodyguards, a friend, Ruth Friedmann,
went to our hotel room and packed our bags. She took with her a small
pouch of personal items that Noleen would not need during our trip.
Two of the bags were to accompany us to London and Copenhagen, and
the third, distinguished by its red color, was to be delivered to Ruth and
Errol Friedmann's home in a Johannesburg suburb.

We arrived at the airport under very heavy security. After being es-
corted to the VIP lounge, we found that our guards had brought all
three suitcases to the airport. Noleen called Ruth Friedmann to ascertain her street address and informed her that our guards would deliver
one suitcase to her after our departure. Ruth told Noleen, somewhat cir-
cumspectly, that she should not worry about the pouch which she had
put into the safe. On delivery, Ruth placed the suitcase in a room con-
taining a number of other suitcases. That night the Friedmann home

was burgled. Only the red suitcase was forced open, however, and its contents strewn around the room. An attempt to break into the safe had been unsuccessful. The keys of Errol's brand-new car were taken by the burglars, who drove off in it. Some days later it was found abandoned, sprayed with bullets from an AK-47. No other contents of their home had been disturbed or stolen. There can be no doubt that Noleen's call to Ruth from the VIP lounge had been tapped by members of the security establishment, who hoped to find useful information in our suitcase and in the safe.

On the flight to London, Noleen and I discussed which hotel the ambassador might have arranged for us. Upon arrival, however, we were requested to leave the aircraft before the other passengers. We were met by an official, Peter, who said he was from the foreign office but who turned out to be a senior officer from one of the British security services. He explained to us that we were not allowed into London and that I would have to interview our witness at a venue "in the country." We were ushered onto the tarmac, where two cars were waiting to drive us to another terminal. En route Peter explained that we were being flown by helicopter to the coast, where we were to be housed in a fortress for the night. I was amazed at the safeguards being taken on our behalf. It would be generous to describe our accommodations as spartan. We had separate single-bunk bedrooms, which I complained about the next morning. Peter informed me that a "safe house" in the country had been arranged for us. We were driven there, somewhere in Wiltshire, the following day. We had pleasant accommodations on a farm. The redeeming feature was the splendid collection of Bordeaux wine that the farmer generously shared with us.

After a few days it became clear to me that the British authorities, for reasons unknown to me, were not happy about my interviewing a commission witness in Britain. Peter was visibly relieved when I suggested that the witness and his family should accompany me to Denmark, where the other witnesses were being kept in safe houses by the Danish police.

When the arrangements were in place, Noleen and I flew to Copenhagen, where, again to our amazement, we were informed that we were to be kept at a hotel outside the city. I then appreciated the fearsome power that criminal elements in the South African security establishment had managed to build up not only in South Africa but also abroad.

During the few days we spent in Denmark, we were looked after by the friendly and efficient Royal Protection Unit. The queen was on holiday in the country, and her guards could not have been more caring and considerate. The Danish government assisted in making all arrangements for me to interview the witnesses. The evidence I obtained was handed to a special unit established under the attorney general of the Transvaal, Dr. Jan d'Oliviera, and eventually led to the successful prosecution of Colonel Eugene de Kock for murder and many other offenses. He received a number of life sentences and is presently awaiting the outcome of his application to the Truth and Reconciliation Commission for amnesty.

Having been through the previous ten days' experiences, it was with considerable nervousness and fear that Noleen and I returned to South Africa. To their credit and courage, the other four members of the commission decided not to ask for special protection during this period, and it is a great relief to me that they suffered no unpleasant consequences.

The evidence that the commission collected during this period more than supported the allegations I had earlier made against senior police officers. It was then about three weeks before our first democratic elections, set for 27 April 1994. De Klerk earnestly requested that I not deliver a further official report in which this evidence would be reported and which he would then have to make public. It was his considered opinion that such disclosure would be certain to cause unrest and jeopardize a peaceful election. I told him that before agreeing to his request I wished to discuss the matter with Mandela. He objected to that on the basis that Mandela was not yet in government. I replied to the effect that very soon he would be. I did discuss de Klerk's request with Mandela, and he shared de Klerk's view. In light of that political judgment by the two men who were really guiding the events in South Africa at that time, I felt there was no option but to comply. I did so on condition that the investigations would proceed and the information would be handed to the unit headed by d'Oliviera. The criminal trials that followed in 1995 and 1996, as well as the work of the Truth and Reconciliation Commission, substantiated all of the allegations made in reports of the commission.

Two of the most serious episodes of violence have never been adequately explained. They were the random and cold-blooded attacks on innocent members of the public who were shot while waiting at taxi stands or traveling in commuter trains. The attackers were usually armed with AK-47s. As with many violent acts at that time, there were a number of rational but contradictory explanations. An obvious possibility was the mysterious third force that wished to disrupt the peace process in this way. Another was that the train killers were hired by dishonest taxi owners who wished to dissuade commuters from using the trains. One of the commissioners, Niel Rossouw, spent many months investigating the taxi violence, some of which was clearly the result of economic wars between rival taxi owners. These problems lasted well after the elections of 1994.

The commission held over forty inquiries. In my view it resulted in three major achievements. The first was that it produced sufficient evidence of serious human rights abuses during the last of the apartheid years to justify the establishment of a truth commission. The second was that its report on senior police involvement in violence as late as 1994 caused substantial disarray within right-wing circles and averted more serious violence in the weeks preceding the April 1994 election. The third, and most important, was that timely public inquiries into serious incidents of violence helped keep the South African nation calm and so avoid a bloody end to the negotiation process that led to the death of apartheid and the birth of a democratic system of government.

It was a great privilege to have been able to play a meaningful role in South Africa's transition from white minority rule to a nonracial democracy. I was struck by the confidence and lack of rancor on the part of our new leaders. They had been given little or no training for government, and many of them had spent years in prison or in exile. The change came far more quickly than any of them could have hoped.

The Goldstone Commission assisted in creating the political climate in which the Truth and Reconciliation Commission could be established with the agreement of the major parties.

The South African Solution: Is Truth Sufficient?

In January 1994, Ruud Lubbers, prime minister of the Netherlands, together with his foreign minister, Pieter Kooijmans, paid an official visit to South Africa, the first ever by a Dutch head of state. At a welcoming reception in Pretoria, President de Klerk remarked that the elections which were to be held some three months later would bring an end to three hundred years of racial oppression in South Africa. Indeed, he added, this situation had prevailed ever since the arrival of the Dutch at the Cape of Good Hope in 1652. I shall always remember the look of acknowledgment, tinged with some embarrassment, on the face of the Dutch prime minister.

In May 1994, a democratically elected South African government had to face an issue common to a number of other governments during the past three decades—how to address grave, systematic human rights abuses committed by their predecessors. Some governments have simply ignored the issue; others have granted blanket amnesties in an endeavor to ensure peace; yet others have prosecuted some of the perpetrators. Some held investigations into past violations and, by making the findings public, provided a form of acknowledgment for the victims.

It is my belief that when nations ignore victims' calls for justice, they are condemning their people to the terrible consequences of ongoing hatred and revenge. I have seen those consequences and their symptoms in a number of different situations. The first relates to my own country and concerns the relationship between the two major white groups—the English and the Afrikaners, who, at the turn of the century, fought the Boer War. All wars leave bitterness and hatred, but for the Afrikaner people, the harshest memories are the deaths of more than twenty-five thousand of their women and children in the British internment camps in South Africa, St. Helena, Bermuda, India, and Ceylon. Whether war crimes were committed by the British was never investigated, and it has remained a closed chapter.

Until I became a judge of the Supreme Court of Appeal, which sits in Bloemfontein, I was not aware of the depth of feeling that this subject evokes in Afrikaner people. Professor Johan Henning, a friend and law professor at the University of the Orange Free State, offered to accompany me on a visit to the Women's Monument and the War Museum. The monument is dedicated to Afrikaner women, who played such an important role in the Great Trek—the movement inland from the Cape of many thousands of Afrikaners who refused to live under British rule. They encountered unimaginable hardships and showed unusual courage, enduring the hazards of nature and attacks from indigenous people who objected to what they, understandably, regarded as an invasion of their lands.

The War Museum records the bravery and the suffering of the Boer forces. A particularly moving section illustrates the death of women and children in the British internment camps. Deeply touched by the exhibits, Professor Henning recounted the victimization of members of his own family. A little known fact is that the expression "concentration camp" dates from that time.

My visit to the War Museum had an almost bizarre sequel at the beginning of 1996, while I was serving in the Netherlands as chief prosecutor of the United Nations Criminal Tribunal. On an official visit to the country, F. W. de Klerk, then deputy-president of South Africa, was invited to a small dinner given in his honor by Queen Beatrix and Prince Claus in The Hague; Noleen and I also attended that evening. De Klerk and I were seated on either side of the queen. Soon after the dinner began, she referred to the state visit she was to make to South Africa later that year. She asked both de Klerk and me whether there was anything special she should consider visiting, since her previous trip had been many years before. De Klerk referred to the wine lands of the Cape and especially Groot Constantia, where the first vines were planted by Governor Simon van der Stel soon after the Dutch arrived at the Cape. She nodded in agreement.

On an impulse, which I soon had cause to regret, I suggested that the queen consider visiting the Women's Monument in Bloemfontein and the War Museum. De Klerk enthusiastically supported that suggestion, adding that she would see for herself how the British, in their concentration camps, had treated Afrikaners similarly to the way the Nazis had treated their victims. The queen reddened visibly, almost rising from her seat, and said: "Mr Deputy President, how dare you say such a thing! How dare you make such a comparison!" De Klerk was stunned. I intervened and said quietly that what Mr. de Klerk had in mind was a difference of degree rather than of substance. Whereas the Nazis had acted with criminal intent, the British had acted with criminal neglect. The queen and de Klerk accepted that rather inadequate explanation as sufficient cause for a truce, and the conversation went in a different direction.

On her visit, the queen did not visit Bloemfontein. Unwittingly and perhaps unthinkingly, de Klerk indicated by his comment that he, together with many Afrikaners, still nurses deep grievances against the British, whose conduct was never investigated. There was no Truth and Reconciliation Commission to hear the experiences of the victims.

In October 1994 I paid my first visit to the former Yugoslavia, where I held meetings with the ministers of foreign affairs and justice in Croatia, Bosnia and Herzegovina, and the Federal Republic of Yugoslavia (the FRY, including Serbia and Montenegro). During the visit to the FRY, the justice minister began our discussion by giving me a very partial history of the relationship between the people of the region. Not surprisingly, he began with the battle of Kosovo, fought in 1389, and eventually worked up to World War II, during which hundreds of thousands of Serbs had been murdered by the Nazi-supporting Ustasha. Cabinet members in both Zagreb and Sarajevo gave me similar history lessons. I need hardly add that the facts and events they recounted had little in common; each referred to his own people's profound feelings of injustice.

In the former Yugoslavia the perpetrators of heinous crimes and human rights abuses were never called to account for their conduct. The historical hate and unanswered calls for justice were allowed to fester and provided fertile material for nationalistic leaders to justify wars of purification—the ethnic cleansing we have come to read about. I was not surprised to find a similar pathology in Rwanda: a history of jealousy and resentment between Hutus and Tutsis that was aggravated by Belgian colonial policy. These conflicts had been the basis of violence over most of the twentieth century and in the middle of 1994 had enabled leaders to mobilize sufficient Hutus to commit horrendous genocide on the Tutsi minority.

When the transition to democracy began in South Africa, I felt it would be a grave error not to have a full accounting of the human rights abuses that had been committed—abuses that went back hundreds of years. The exclusion of black South Africans from 87 percent of the land in the country of their ancestors was legislated in 1913. The indignities blacks suffered as a consequence of racial discrimination and oppression went back long before it was systematized and given the official title of apartheid in 1948. There was no question in my mind that to ignore the victimization of the great majority of South Africans would be a recipe for escalating enmity between the races.

During the transition period, which began in 1990, stories about the ill treatment of ANC members in their own camps in Angola and elsewhere began to emerge. The ANC appointed two commissions of inquiry into these allegations, and findings of serious human rights abuses emerged. My colleague on the Constitutional Court of South Africa, Justice Albie Sachs, has told me that it was in light of those findings that the leadership of the ANC, in his presence, first considered a truth commission for postapartheid South Africa. "If we are looking at our own human rights record," they reasoned, "on what possible basis should there be a national amnesia in respect of the record of the apartheid regime?"

At about the same time, Dr. Alex Boraine, a former opposition member of Parliament and then the national director of the Institute for a Democratic Alternative for South Africa (IDASA), began his own truth commission initiative. He, too, was convinced that national amnesia was unacceptable and, after extensive consultations, organized two important seminars in Cape Town. He received strong support from the Open Society Fund of George Soros and from Dr. Jorge Heine, the Chilean ambassador to South Africa.[1] As chairperson of the Goldstone Commission, I was invited to attend both seminars. Our investigations of systematic political violence, some of which was sponsored from within the state's security forces, were highly relevant to the issues facing the seminar participants.

One of the participants in the second seminar was Patricio Aylwin, the former president of Chile, who in 1990 had set up a National Commission on Truth and Reconciliation in his own country. That commission held its inquiries behind closed doors and in its report named none of the perpetrators of gross human rights abuses, its mandate having been limited to "disappearances." General Augusto Pinochet, head of the army, had imposed those limitations so as not to have an all-out campaign against his own men. Notwithstanding those serious constraints upon the commission, Chile's experience was positive. The report was formally handed to President Aylwin on national television, at which time he apologized to his nation for the terrible deeds of predecessor governments. That report and the manner in which it was treated substantially helped Chile on its road to reconciliation and democracy.

In addition to President Aylwin, two leaders of the ANC actively participated in the Cape Town seminar: Dullah Omar, previously minister of justice, now minister of transport, and Kader Asmal, previously minister of water affairs and forestry, now minister for education. They were among the main protagonists for a South African truth commission. Four South African victims of apartheid were invited to talk about their experiences. One of them was Albie Sachs, who spoke of the trauma of having an arm and an eye blown away by a bomb that South African agents had placed under his car in Maputo, the capital of Mozambique. Then came the turn of Mrs. Gcina, the widow of a small-town lawyer whose only political activity was representing community leaders who were brought to court under draconian apartheid security laws. She spoke of how the security police had terrorized her and their young children with midnight raids and repeated detentions of her husband. One day after the police had taken away her husband for the final time, she heard on the radio that his bullet-riddled body had been found in a field some distance from their home. When Mrs. Gcina described how her twelve-year-old son came to her and asked when his father would be home, her composure dissolved and she began to weep. No one who was present will forget the scene of Albie Sachs attempting to console Mrs. Gcina with the stump of his right arm.

The point of the story arises from the conversation I had with Mrs. Gcina the following morning at breakfast. I complimented her on her courage in coming to speak of her experiences. She responded by expressing her gratitude for having been able to do so: "You know, Judge, last night was the first night since I lost my husband that I have slept through and not been awakened by nightmares." When I asked her how she explained that, she responded without a moment's hesitation: "There were so many important people here who were interested in hearing my story." Any doubts I had about the healing effect of the public acknowledgment of the suffering of victims were resolved at that moment.

My experience in The Hague has taught me that the same healing effect can also come about through a credible judicial process. We needed evidence of war crimes committed against innocent civilians near the town of Tuzla, in Bosnia and Herzegovina. Our investigators approached some of the victims there, and as was our experience elsewhere with victims, they needed no persuading. They wished to testify not only on their own behalf but also on behalf of other victims. Ten witnesses, men and women, were chosen to testify before the Yugoslavia tribunal. They were given the option of testifying with or without the disclosure of their identities. All but one insisted on giving evidence openly so that they could be identified by their families and friends. The one who chose otherwise did so not for himself but for close family members he feared would be the subject of reprisals.

The ten witnesses arrived as a disparate and unhappy group, depressed and bewildered by the strange environment in which they found themselves. All were under witness protection, and their freedom of movement was therefore severely restricted. They bickered among themselves, and some required medical and psychological intervention. I met them on the day they arrived in The Hague and saw them again a couple of weeks later, after they had testified. The change in their demeanor before and after was remarkable: they returned home a happier and more united group of people. By publicly exposing their own suffering and that of their families and friends, they had significantly contributed to the tribunal. They, like Mrs. Gcina, had received acknowledgment from a credible public forum.

While the leaders of the ANC and people like Alex Boraine were becoming more convinced that South Africa should have an official truth commission, de Klerk and his government and the ruling National Party were becoming more convinced that the less investigation into the past, the better. If they had had their way, a blanket amnesty would have been granted for all crimes committed prior to 1994. Of course, if Mandela and the ANC leaders could have had their way, they would have opted for Nuremberg-style trials for the former apartheid leaders. The eventual agreement to establish the Truth and Reconciliation Commission (TRC), therefore, was a political compromise. It is generally accepted that the revelations of the Goldstone Commission, particularly those implicating the leaders of the South African Police and the military, made it more difficult for de Klerk to resist the ANC demand for some form of accounting.

The second IDASA seminar included experts from Argentina, Uruguay, Chile, El Salvador, Poland, Hungary, Germany, Bulgaria, and the Czech Republic. I chaired the final session, in which consideration was given to an appropriate South African response. Before introducing the speakers, I offered the following comments:

This conference has been an intellectually stimulating but emotionally draining experience for the South Africans attending. To look at the problems of justice in transition simply from a moral point of view is difficult in itself. To do so from a jurisprudential or theological perspective would be similarly difficult. Add to that the political dimension and the task of finding a solution that will satisfy most of those who need to be satisfied seems almost insurmountable.

The attendance here of South Africans who are all but consumed with the present constitutional and political events leading up to the April election is a proper indication of the importance with which South Africans do regard and need to regard this topic. If a new government shies away from the subject it will do so at its own peril and that of all our people.[2]

The establishment of the Truth and Reconciliation Commission was anticipated by a provision at the end of the interim Constitution, which was in force from 27 April 1994 until it was replaced by the final Constitution, on 7 February 1997. In what is often called a postamble, the interim Constitution states:

This Constitution provides a historic bridge between the past of a deeply divided society characterised by strife, conflict, untold suffering and injustice, and a future founded on the recognition of human rights, democracy and peaceful co-existence and development opportunities for all South Africans, irrespective of colour, race, class, belief or sex.

The pursuit of national unity, the well-being of all South African citizens and peace require reconciliation between the people of South Africa and the reconstruction of society.

The adoption of this Constitution lays the secure foundation for the people of South Africa to transcend the divisions and strife of the past, which generated gross violations of human rights, the transgression of humanitarian principles in violent conflicts and a legacy of hatred, fear, guilt and revenge.

These can now be addressed on the basis that there is a need for understanding but not for vengeance, a need for reparation but not for retaliation, a need for *ubuntu* [humanity] but not victimization.

In order to advance such reconciliation and reconstruction, amnesty shall be granted in respect of acts, omissions and offences associated with political objectives and committed in the course of the conflicts of the past. To this end, Parliament under this Constitution shall adopt a law determining a firm cut-off date . . . and providing for the mechanisms, criteria and procedures, including tribunals, if any, through which such amnesty shall be dealt with at any time after the law has been passed.

Pursuant to that provision, the South African Parliament, with the support of a substantial majority of its members, passed the Promotion of National Unity and Reconciliation Act in 1995. In terms thereof, the TRC was charged with a number of duties. One was to establish as complete a picture as possible of the causes, nature, and extent of the human rights abuses committed from 1 March 1960 until 27 April 1994, the date of the first democratic election.[3] Another duty of the TRC was to grant amnesty to persons who made full disclosure of all facts relating to acts associated with a political objective.

Three committees of the TRC were established under the statute: the Committee on Human Rights Abuses, charged with investigating gross violations of human rights during the relevant period; the Committee on Amnesty, charged with considering and ruling on amnesty applications made to the TRC; and the Reparations Committee, charged with considering appropriate reparations for the victims of the human rights violations.

A person granted amnesty is not only protected from criminal prosecution for the acts in question but also has immunity from civil actions for damages. Some victims challenged the constitutionality of the amnesty provisions under the interim Constitution, but their objections were eventually dismissed by the Constitutional Court.[4]

I played no role with regard to the work of the TRC, in that it was established and began its work while I was in The Hague. In any event, I would clearly have been disqualified from any active involvement, because I had an ax to grind: I had made findings in a number of important areas that were clearly to be investigated by the TRC. In addition, I would not have been considered impartial—in fact I would not have been impartial. It was important to me that the findings of my Commission, many of which were strenuously denied, be confirmed by the TRC.

It was inevitable that the Truth and Reconciliation Commission would be a controversial body. Given its wide mandate, it was bound to make decisions and findings that would anger one party or another. Indeed it ended up upsetting virtually all parties. That was best illustrated during the week it issued its final report. A couple of days before, former president de Klerk, having been informed of findings against him, had approached the High Court for an order prohibiting the TRC from publishing the report. He complained that the allegations were based on incorrect facts and that he had not been afforded an opportunity to deal with them. Rather than hold up a report of some thirty-five hundred pages, the TRC agreed to delete, provisionally, the offending passages, which occupied less than a page of the text. This was a pointless exercise, however, because the passages had already been leaked to and published by the media. Then, on 28 October 1998, the very day of the planned release, the African National Congress received a short summary of the report and came to the conclusion that it, too, had been unfairly dealt with. It also approached the High Court for an urgent order stopping the release of the entire report. The TRC successfully opposed the application of the ANC, and the report was released by its chairperson, Archbishop Desmond Tutu. That the report incurred the wrath of both the ANC and the National Party is a good indication that it represented a balanced presentation.

The work of the TRC was widely publicized by the South African media. Many of its hearings were televised and broadcast live to the nation on radio and television, and its activities were covered in almost all news bulletins. In my view, its most signal success is that the evidence it amassed of gross abuses during the apartheid era has made it literally impossible for those abuses to be credibly denied. The refrain I heard from a substantial number of white people during the last year or so of the TRC's work was that there had been "more than enough of re-opening wounds." "Whose wounds are they?" I would inquire. "Surely not yours. And what makes you think that those wounds have ever healed?" Many letters to the press complained about the work of the commission and alleged that it was achieving not reconciliation but the opposite. The victims' most serious complaint was that the perpetrators were not being brought to justice and were being allowed by the TRC process to escape any meaningful punishment. Some also charged that the TRC was not providing them with appropriate reparations.

During 1997 I shared a platform at Duke University with Ariel Dorfman, the Chilean playwright and author of the wonderful play *Death and the Maiden*. After I suggested that white complainers were not the victims, Dorfman, in response, pointed out that white people in South Africa were also victims of apartheid. They had been forced to acknowledge the terrible crimes committed against the black majority and had to live with their consciences. Of course, his analysis is valid.

José Zalaquett, the Chilean human rights activist and a member of the Chilean Commission on Truth and Reconciliation, has written in moving terms about the victims in his country and how the work of the commission has affected this abused group: "The relatives of the victims showed great generosity. Of course, many of them asked for justice. Hardly anyone, however, showed a desire for vengeance. Most of them stressed that in the end, what really mattered to them was that the truth be revealed, that the memory of their loved ones not be denigrated or forgotten, and that such things never happen again."[5] Those words could well have been written by a member of the TRC.

South Africa was fortunate in having had the resources to afford a sophisticated truth commission and in investing it with far-reaching powers. The new South African government, under the leadership of Mandela, was firmly in power after the 1994 elections, and security forces were rapidly being subordinated to civil authority. This explains why the hearings were public, why the names of perpetrators were published, and why the commission was able by its empowering statute to compel the evidence of witnesses and the production of private and public documents.

The South African Truth and Reconciliation Commission nonetheless remained a high-risk affair. Many feared that it would be ignored and that it would not enjoy the support of the broad population. Fortunately those fears proved to be without substance. More than twenty thousand victims gave evidence to the Committee on Human Rights Abuses, and more than eight thousand applications for amnesty were received by the Amnesty Committee.

It will take many decades for the effects of the TRC's activities and recommendations to be appropriately analyzed and appreciated. In my opinion, however, it can safely be said that South Africa is a better country in light of the accomplishments of the Truth and Reconciliation Commission. But for the TRC, there would have been widespread denials of most of the worst manifestations of apartheid, and those denials would have been believed and accepted by the majority of white South Africans. That is no longer possible. Nor could the same result have been achieved through the normal criminal process. It would have taken scores of long and costly trials to have recorded the history of the human rights abuses perpetrated during the apartheid era. The commission has made many recommendations, and it will be important for the South African Parliament to debate them fully and to implement the most significant of them.

My relationship with the Truth and Reconciliation Commission was tangential, and it should be left to those who were intimately involved in the process to tell its story. Suffice it for me to state here my great admiration for the awesome task it performed during its thirty-month existence. I have no doubt that South Africans will live to appreciate its work and legacy.

Leading figures of the TRC have launched a new, nongovernmental organization in order to further some of its uncompleted work. It is also hoped that this organization will be able to assist other countries interested in the truth-commission process. One such country is Bosnia and Herzegovina. A significant number of people in that country are talking about a truth commission as a means of encouraging reconciliation between the three major groups: the Muslims, the Serbs, and the Croats. It is generally acknowledged that all three groups have committed serious human rights abuses.

Although the relationship between such a truth-commission process and the Yugoslavia tribunal is not a simple one, I have no doubt that any problems could be resolved. For example, such a commission should not be empowered to grant amnesties for war crimes. Its purpose should be to provide a credible platform from which victims on all sides could tell their stories. This would require an efficient and effective investigation department to ensure that so-called victims were not able to use the platform for the propagation of fabricated evidence. A system would also be required whereby the Office of the Prosecutor would be given prior notice of the witnesses and the evidence so as to determine which evidence would anticipate and prejudice a pending tribunal proceeding. A form of truth commission for Bosnia, as has been the case in South Africa, would enable a more accurate history of the war to be recorded. The centuries of hate in that explosive region have only been exacerbated, because each group has nurtured its subjective grievances and victims have never been acknowledged in any public way.

South Africa has the opportunity of repaying the international community for the many ways it helped bring about the death of apartheid by sharing its experiences of the past decade.

International Justice: The United Nations Criminal
Tribunals for the Former Yugoslavia and Rwanda

Toward the end of July 1994 I was elected by the Security Council as chief prosecutor of the Yugoslavia tribunal in The Hague. That week, the former British prime minister Edward Heath was on a private yachting holiday in Cape Town. Sir Anthony Reeve, the British ambassador, invited me to a small party to meet Heath. When I arrived, the ambassador mentioned to Heath that I had just been appointed to prosecute war crimes in the former Yugoslavia. "Why did you accept such a ridiculous job?" Heath asked me in a friendly tone. I told him that I thought prosecuting war criminals was important, especially given the magnitude of crimes allegedly committed in Bosnia. Heath replied to the effect that if people wished to murder one another, as long as they did not do so in his country, it was not his concern and should not be the concern of the British government. At the time his opinion startled me. Little did I realize that he was candidly stating what many leading politicians in major Western nations were saying privately — and what many of them still believe.

The few days I had before leaving for briefings at the United Nations headquarters in New York were taken up with reading as much material on the former Yugoslavia as I could find. I knew little about prosecuting and even less about the history of Yugoslavia. I had read much of the Nuremberg trials over the years but little about their Japanese counterpart. And to have described my knowledge of international humanitarian law as scanty would have been generous.

When I look around my library today, I am taken aback at how many books I read during those first few months. In particular, I found the history of humanitarian law to be fascinating and began to understand the importance of the legacy of the Nuremberg trials. Not only were they the first serious attempt to bring war criminals to account for their conduct, but they ushered in a completely new era in international law.

Prior to World War II, the subjects of international law were not individuals but nations. Individual human beings had no standing. But the Holocaust changed that. It was a change first manifested in the London Agreement of 8 August 1945, which established the military tribunal at Nuremberg and recognized a new offense: the "crime against humanity." It was the first time in legal history that certain crimes were identified as being of such a magnitude that they injured not only the immediate victims and not only the people in the country or on the continent where they were committed but also all of humankind. It was the first formal recognition of a universal jurisdiction over certain heinous crimes.[1] People who committed crimes against humanity could be brought to account by courts, both national and international, regardless of where the crimes were committed and regardless of the nationality of the perpetrators or their victims.

That universal jurisdiction was formally recognized by the General Assembly of the United Nations when, in 1946, it unanimously affirmed the substantive principles of the Nuremberg Charter and judgment. Universal jurisdiction for particularly serious war crimes was also accepted by the international community in 1949 with the adoption of the four Geneva Conventions of that year. Those conventions, which have been ratified by almost all of the members of the United

Nations, oblige all States Parties to prosecute, in their own courts, anyone who commits a "grave breach." Alternatively, if such Parties are unwilling to prosecute them, they are obliged to deliver these individuals to a Party prepared to bring them to trial. One finds a similar universal jurisdiction in the Convention on the Suppression and Punishment of the Crime of Apartheid of 1973 and the Convention against Torture and Other Cruel, Inhuman or Degrading Treatment or Punishment of 1984.

Nuremberg also introduced individual criminal responsibility for war crimes and individualized the guilt of Nazi leaders. This was an innovative development allowing for distinction and differentiation—significant in a context where not all were responsible for the atrocities and those responsible were not equally to blame. As I remarked at a commemoration of the fiftieth anniversary of the trials, the emotive photographs of Nazi leaders in the dock showed them for what they were—a group of criminals who could not be said to represent the German people as a whole. Although the democratically elected leaders of the Third Reich pillaged the ideals of humanity, Germany has also produced the likes of Beethoven, Goethe, and Schiller, who have affirmed humankind's best impulses. During the Nuremberg trials, important history of the Third Reich was formally recorded, much of it through the contents of official Nazi documents. But for that, the work of those who denied the Holocaust would have been substantially fulfilled.

Soon after my appointment by the Security Council, I was invited to visit New York and The Hague to be briefed on my work. By the time I reached New York my enthusiasm had been fired by my readings and by the messages of support I had received from both friends and strangers. Human rights activists in the United States were particularly encouraging in response to my appointment, as was Archbishop Desmond Tutu, whose letter of congratulations was written in the most supportive and warm terms. I particularly appreciated a friendly letter from Simon Wiesenthal, the famous "Nazi hunter," who referred to the importance of the work I had been appointed to do. He invited me to call on him if ever I visited Vienna. I later took him up on that invitation.

What began to concern me were the negative views that people expressed about working within the United Nations system. I had assumed that a United Nations tribunal, which was a suborgan of the Security Council itself and established by the unanimous vote of its members, would be adequately funded and well supported by the international body. That, unfortunately, turned out to be a naive assumption. I remember my surprise when I was told after arriving in New York that the funding for my visit there and to The Hague had not yet been approved. I could not be reimbursed in New York, as previously informed; I would have to await payment in The Hague. At the request of the Office of Legal Affairs I had paid the air fare out of my own pocket.

My meeting in New York with the secretary-general, Boutros Boutros-Ghali, was particularly cordial. He assured me of his full support and that of his Secretariat. His spokesperson arranged a press conference for me and suggested that I hold one in The Hague as well. Both conferences proved a difficult start to my new relationship with the international media, which effectively had written off the International Criminal Tribunal for the former Yugoslavia (ICTY) as the "fig leaf" of the international community established to hide its shame for inaction in the former Yugoslavia, particularly in Bosnia. There was little I could say to change that negative attitude. I did give the assurance that I would do all I could to ensure that investigations into war crimes would begin as soon as possible and that I would keep the media well informed of our progress. During my work in South Africa, I had had the advantage of coming into contact with many foreign journalists, a relationship that proved cordial and constructive. I am fortunate too in always having enjoyed talking to and working with journalists.

During the visit to New York, I was also invited to have a short meeting with the Security Council. The procedure was the same as it had been when I met with the council in 1993. By an amazing coincidence the president of the council that month was again Ambassador Jamsheed Marker, of Pakistan, who was as friendly as I remembered him on the previous occasion. Pakistan was a firm supporter of the tribunal and quickly contributed $1 million to the special trust fund for the tribunal established by the secretary-general. The fact that Muslims in Bosnia were the victims of ethnic cleansing obviously elicited the support of most Islamic governments.

Again, I was warmly welcomed by Madeleine Albright, who had played the leading role in having the tribunal established. Her continued support for the work of the Yugoslavia tribunal, and later the Rwanda tribunal, was crucial to their success. She appointed one of her senior advisers, David Scheffer, to take special responsibility for moving the work of the tribunal forward. David became a friend and adviser to me, especially with regard to my contacts with the various branches of the United States administration. His commitment to the work of both tribunals was deep and supportive.

From the outset, one of the questions I was asked was why the Security Council had established a war crimes tribunal for the former Yugoslavia and had not done so in the case of Cambodia or Iraq or any of the other equally serious conflicts in Africa or Asia. After discussion with experts in the field, I soon became convinced that the Security Council acted on Yugoslavia because of a convergence of circumstances in the middle of 1993:

1. The justified description of the Serbian policy in Bosnia as ethnic cleansing recalled terrible memories of the Holocaust.

2. Images of Bosnia, reinforced by emotive photographs of emaciated Bosnian camp inmates that were seen around the world via satellite, were reminiscent of World War II concentration camps.

3. Politically abhorrent events were taking place in Europe that the European powers had assumed could never happen again.

4. National and international human rights organizations had recently acquired the power to influence public opinion and, therefore, governmental policies in a number of important democracies. It should be noted that when Amnesty International or Human Rights Watch issue damning reports on human rights violations in any part of the world, governments take notice and respond. And in many countries local organizations now play an increasing role in monitoring and publicizing human rights abuses.

5. The Security Council had already determined that the situation in the former Yugoslavia was a threat to international peace and security and so triggered its peremptory peace-keeping powers under Chapter 7 of the United Nations Charter.

6. The Commission of Experts that the Security Council had set up some months earlier had provided evidence of the most nightmarish of war crimes.

7. The establishment of an international criminal tribunal had long been envisaged by international lawyers as a means of enforcing human rights and suppressing international crimes. Mention is made of such a tribunal as far back as 1948, in the Genocide Convention, but dissent triggered by the Cold War precluded any agreement on the tribunal. The end of the Cold War, however, allowed the Security Council, with the agreement of Russia and China, to establish an ad hoc war crimes tribunal for the former Yugoslavia.

8. The traditionally accepted method of establishing an international criminal tribunal, by treaty, would have been too laborious and time-

consuming and would not have bound nations that refused to ratify the treaty, in particular countries that had been constituents of the former Yugoslavia.

At the press conferences I held, both in New York and The Hague, I was questioned about the role I had played in South Africa during its transition to democracy. I emphasized, in that context, the importance I attached to my appointment as a member of the first South African Constitutional Court and mentioned the two-year leave of absence I had been granted from that court. This became an issue when I left the tribunal at the end of September 1996.

After my meetings in New York, I spent three days at the tribunal in The Hague. I was met at the Amsterdam airport by Graham Blewitt, an experienced Australian prosecutor who had been appointed as acting deputy prosecutor by Ramon Escovar-Salom of Venezuela, during his few days in The Hague as chief prosecutor. The statute of the tribunal did not provide for such a post, but I shall be forever grateful to Escovar-Salom for having taken that action.

Blewitt and I became firm friends and worked well together from the time of our first meeting. He had already assembled about forty people in the office, twenty-three from the United States, five from Australia, and the others from an assortment of other countries. I had the distinct impression that Blewitt was concerned that I might wish to reorganize the Office of the Prosecutor. Nothing was further from my mind. In addition to his ability as a prosecutor and lawyer, Blewitt is exceptionally gifted in office management. He therefore played a crucial role in areas in which I was inexperienced.

The many delays and inefficiencies that dogged the ICTY in its first few years have been well documented. Although many problems were of the sort endemic to any large bureaucratic organization, others stemmed directly from the United Nations' lack of experience in the field of criminal justice. The International Court of Justice in The Hague was no prototype, since only governments appear as parties before that court, and it has no criminal jurisdiction. The rules of the United Nations simply do not apply to the staffing and running of a tribunal expected to investigate and prosecute war crimes against individual perpetrators.

I began my term of office on 15 August 1994. My first appointment that morning was a television interview with Mike Wallace of "60 Minutes." I had been warned that he was one of the most experienced and difficult television interviewers and that I should be particularly careful and say as little as possible. These dire warnings caused me much anxiety and many hours of lost sleep. Although the interview was not calculated to make the work of the ICTY easier, I found Wallace friendly, polite, and sympathetic. The program, titled "An Exercise in Hypocrisy?" castigated the United Nations and the international community for the manner in which it was treating the tribunal. It ended with a couple of minutes of Wallace talking to me, and that short sequence enabled me to inject an optimistic, if muted, note.

Many months later, I agreed to a second session with Wallace after he returned from Pale, where he had conducted a long interview with Radovan Karadžić, then president of the Bosnian Serb Republic of Srpska. Unable to interview me personally in The Hague, Wallace arranged a satellite link. As we began to speak, however, his television monitor in New York developed technical difficulties, and we chatted for about fifteen minutes while the technicians repaired the fault. At one point Wallace made a statement with which I agreed. When he asked me if I had nodded my agreement while he was talking, I said that indeed I had done so. He then cautioned me to be more careful in such situations: the cameras had been rolling, and he could use my taped nod to indicate my approval of any statement he cared to make!

On that first day a serious crisis was awaiting my arrival. The twenty-three Americans working in the office included lawyers, computer technicians, and police investigators, all of whom had been assigned to the tribunal by the U.S. government, at no cost to the United Nations. The United States had taken that action in an attempt to jump-start the Office of the Prosecutor and so make up for the slowness and inefficiencies at the United Nations headquarters in New York. The Americans were performing essential services that had enabled the initial investigations to begin even before my arrival. According to United Nations rules, however, gifts of any kind, whether material or human resources, from a member state to any United Nations operation were required to be accompanied by a cash subvention equal to 13 percent of the cost of the grant to the donor nation. This arbitrary percentage is intended to pay for any unbudgeted costs the United Nations may incur because of the grant. Because all U.N. members have a vote on the budget, it would be unacceptable if any one member, by making a gift, forced the organization to incur expenditure for which no budgetary provision had been made. In the case of the Office of the Prosecutor, the personnel had been given offices, computers, and secretarial assistance, and the investigators had begun to incur travel expenses.

The United States, according to the 13 percent clause, was required to pay more than $1 million to support these activities but had refused to do so, having adopted the attitude that this was a special case and that the rule should be waived. The Secretariat in New York was adamant in its refusal to comply with the demand. As a result, these costs were being met from regular United Nations funding, which had not been authorized by the other member states. In response to the United

States' refusal, an order had been issued in New York to the effect that no more monies were to be expended on U.S. personnel. Consequently, the investigators were no longer able to travel and had no work to perform.

I had no doubt that the future of the tribunal, and especially its credibility, demanded a rapid and favorable resolution to this problem. To achieve this, I decided to arrange meetings in Washington, D.C., and New York. My first meeting, in Washington, was with Conrad Harper, the legal adviser at the State Department, and thus began a warm friendship. He is not only an astute but, above all, a warm and generous man who wholeheartedly supported the work of the tribunal. Notwithstanding that support, Harper made it clear to me that on this issue the State Department was not prepared to make any concessions. I then made urgent appeals to senior financial officials of the U.N. in an effort to resolve the impasse. I must confess that I also let it be known that if the crisis was not satisfactorily resolved, I intended to make a public protest. Whether or not that precipitated the solution, I do not know, but United Nations officials quickly agreed that the rule would be waived and that the United States would be excused from paying its cash contribution. The following year the rule was again waived. In the third year, however, shortly after Louise Arbour took over as chief prosecutor, no such waiver was forthcoming from New York, and she had to suffer the consequences of the withdrawal of valuable United States personnel.

My contact with Conrad Harper proved useful many months later when we wanted to use as evidence some aired footage of CNN International. One of our investigators had contacted individuals in the head office of CNN in Atlanta, but they were unhappy at the prospect of providing us footage, even though it had been used in a news bulletin. Eventually I contacted a senior executive who agreed to meet our request, but only on the condition that a subpoena from the tribunal be served on CNN. The film was required urgently for a proceeding in The Hague courtroom a few weeks later. The problem was that if the subpoena was sent through diplomatic channels, it might take weeks to get to CNN. I called Harper and explained my problem. He said he would consult his colleagues in the Justice Department and within an hour called me back. He asked whether the subpoena could possibly result in any court proceedings, either in the United States or in The Hague. There was no possibility of that, I assured him, and offered to give him a guarantee to that effect. In that case, he said, there was no objection to the subpoena being served on CNN informally, which involved simply faxing a copy of the document to Atlanta that day. Within days we had the desired film in The Hague. That sort of cooperation is simply not possible without personal contact and a relationship of mutual trust.

It was during that visit that I again met with Aryeh Neier, the head of George Soros's Open Society Fund. I had previously met him in Cape Town, where both of us participated in the seminars that preceded the establishment of the Truth and Reconciliation Commission.[2] At the meeting in New York, Neier informed me that the Open Society Fund had made three hundred thousand dollars available for the tribunal and that I should let him know when it was needed. Many months later I discovered the value of such a resource outside the United Nations financial system. I first called on that fund to buy radio transmitters and receivers for our investigators, who were working in a dangerous part of Bosnia. To have purchased them through the United Nations system would have taken some weeks. For security reasons, we needed them immediately. I called Neier in New York, and within forty-eight hours the equipment was delivered to our investigators in Bosnia. As the availability of that fund indicates, George Soros was himself firmly committed to the work of the tribunal. Some months after that incident, he hosted a reception for three of the tribunal's judges and me at his Manhattan residence. A number of the people I met on that occasion were later helpful to me in my work as chief prosecutor.

Other nongovernmental organizations (NGOs) also played a significant role in supporting the work of both the Yugoslavia and Rwanda tribunals. Soon after I arrived in The Hague, I was besieged by thousands of letters and petitions signed by people, mostly women, from many countries, urging me to give adequate attention to gender-related war crimes. They pointed to the many reports of systematic mass rape in Bosnia and to the glaring inadequacies of humanitarian law in dealing with that crime. I was grateful to those people and organizations, who made me more sensitive to the issue and more determined to do something about it. It led, among other things, to my appointing Patricia Sellars, a thoughtful international lawyer from the United States, as my special adviser on gender, both in our office and in relation to our investigations and indictments. I believed that if we failed to deal appropriately with gender matters within the Office of the Prosecutor, we would be ill equipped to deal with them properly in our investigations and indictments. It has been a matter of particular satisfaction to me that systematic mass rape has now been held by the Rwanda tribunal to constitute a war crime.

Graham Blewitt was required to spend many days at irritating and time-consuming meetings with United Nations officials in obtaining agreement on the levels at which the prosecutor's staff would be employed. One example concerns the three senior trial attorneys we decided to take on. We required that they have trial and prosecuting experience and be able to try cases before the two trial chambers and argue the cases that would inevitably come before the appeals chamber. The issue was whether the level of this post in the United Nations grading system should be P5 or D1. Blewitt and I considered that the terms of employment associated with the higher DI posts were appropriate. Agreement to our request was withheld, however, because of the effect that such a decision might have on the many hundreds, if not thousands, of other lawyers employed in the United Nations system. Most of them had worked their way up the ladder and would have complained about hiring newcomers at such senior positions. Although this concern was obviously serious in the larger context of the United Nations, it had little to do with our work.

The secretary-general delegated his hiring and firing authority with respect to tribunal staff to the registrar of the tribunal. This led to unfortunate problems and difficulties that were exacerbated by unimaginative and sometimes malicious officials who had been seconded to the tribunal from other United Nations offices in order to advise the registrar. When I left, after twenty-eight months in office, some of the difficulties had still not been resolved.

A more serious problem arose from the fact that an official in the registrar's office was responsible for approving all travel claims by officials of the tribunal. Again, this included the Office of the Prosecutor. In most cases the claims were routine and occasioned no difficulty. But there were cases in which members of my office, usually investigators, were required to go on highly confidential missions and the reasons for their travel could obviously not be disclosed. In a few cases, for security reasons, we were not even prepared to disclose the country involved. Fortunately, the registrar and the senior member of her staff responsible for approving travel claims were sympathetic and understood the delicate nature of such trips. As a solution, they were willing to accept my assurance that such travel was necessary and justified; without that arrangement, insuperable difficulties would have arisen. Clearly this position was not acceptable, because the authority to approve travel in the prosecutor's office should have rested with a senior official in that office. What the position is today in this regard I do not know. In any event, this matter should be taken into consideration when the international criminal court is eventually established.

Many of these problems would probably not have arisen but for the critical financial position in which the United Nations has found itself in consequence of the United States being so substantially in arrears in its dues. One related incident caused me much personal anguish. I had accepted an invitation from the city of Nuremberg to address a seminar commemorating the fiftieth anniversary of the start of the Nuremberg trials. The opening was to take place in the very courtroom where the trial of the major Nazi leaders was held in 1945. About two days prior to the event, the personal assistant of the secretary-general called to say that Boutros-Ghali had instructed me not to attend the seminar, though no reason was given for this unusual message. On no account, however, was I willing to let down the organizers of the seminar. I asked to speak to the secretary-general, but he was not available. I informed his assistant that I was not prepared to accept the instruction—if that is what it was—and that he should arrange for me to speak to the secretary-general directly. His assistant agreed to have him call me that evening. I remember well the tense wait before the call came through. When Boutros-Ghali came on the line, I inquired about the reason for his message. The financial crisis at the United Nations, he explained, had left him no choice but to cancel all travel by officials. I then told him that my travel was being paid for by the city of Nuremberg. "Oh," he said, "in that case there is no problem about your attending the seminar." I had no doubt that a member of the administrative staff in the registrar's office had provided Boutros-Ghali's office with incomplete details of my trip. That no one had checked with me or any of my assistants to ascertain the correct facts was not an unusual occurrence.

Some months later the United Nations Secretariat again found it necessary to stop all travel by their officials. That ruling, we were told, applied to all persons working for the tribunal. I could not accept this ruling for our investigators. If they were unable to travel, they simply could not do their work. At that time there was in excess of $10 million in the special trust fund the secretary-general had set up for the Yugoslavia tribunal. I suggested to the financial officials in New York that we use the unearmarked funds for the travel expenses of our investigators. After a few days I was informed that the funds were not available, and my request for an explanation went unanswered. Later that week, over lunch with the Pakistani ambassador to The Hague, I mentioned my problem and suggested that the permanent representative of Pakistan to the United Nations make an inquiry to the Secretariat about the availability of money in the trust fund. I pointed out that Pakistan had every right to do so in that it had donated $1 million to the fund. The ambassador conveyed my request to the permanent representative in New York, who followed through. Whether that played a role in releasing the funds I do not know, but within a day or two the monies I had requested were made available.

I now turn to a number of other issues that impinge on the office of the prosecutor. That his or her duties cannot be appropriately fulfilled without an absolute guarantee of independence is little appreciated, especially in nonlegal quarters. As chairperson of the Goldstone Commission in South Africa, I could not have carried out my responsibilities had I not been allowed absolute autonomy. The fact that I was a judge of the highest court facilitated the exercise of that independence. So too did the fact that the political leaders on all sides respected my position of complete neutrality.

Operating in an international environment makes the question of independence more complex, which was one of the reasons I was determined to use my title of Justice. The title would, in my opinion, attract more respect for the Office of the Prosecutor and result in a greater recognition of my independence. A few of the tribunal judges raised the petty objection that addressing the prosecutor as "Justice" would cause public confusion. The general rule in the United Nations is that titles are ignored. One can sympathize with that rule in light of the complexities and confusions that would arise if national titles were retained by officials of the organization. In my case, however, the Protocol Committee of the United Nations ruled that it was appropriate and permissible to retain the title. My successor, Justice Louise Arbour, has followed the same practice, and certainly for the same reason.

The relationship between the tribunal's judges and the prosecutor's office has been a complicated and sometimes unhappy one. Given the different systems from which we all came, this was perhaps unavoidable. In the Anglo-American tradition the functions of judge and prosecutor are clearly separated. This is not so in civil-law systems, where investigating judges play a leading role in criminal investigations and work closely with the prosecutor.

When I arrived in The Hague, the judges, as I have already mentioned, were frustrated and angry at the fact that they had no work to do. They anticipated that I would keep them informed of the policy I was adopting with regard to investigations and expected regular updates from me. By the time my term of office was coming to an end, the only trial under way was that of Dusan Tadić.[3] In other words, the tribunal was not really in a trial mode. For that reason, I decided that there was no real prejudice to anyone if I provided the judges with some information on progress in my office. (I was not without misgivings, however; I did not want the judges to interfere with the policy or work of the prosecutor, and I worried that their involvement with my office might lead to embarrassing applications for their recusal at a later stage.) When the trials really got under way, my successor was in office, and I fear that I may have left her with the problem of having to create the appropriate distance between herself and her staff and the judges.

Soon after I began my work, it became clear that obtaining intelligence information from Washington would be important. I had certainly not anticipated the intense sensitivity of the United States administration with regard to sharing such information. The late Arthur Liman, in his *Lawyer: A Life of Counsel and Controversy*, provides a good illustration of this.[4] He tells of an incident that arose soon after he was appointed as counsel to the Senate Committee investigating the Iran-Contra affair:

> Still another problem was that every pertinent document we needed was classified, even some that had been printed in the *Washington Post*. Every member of my staff would require a top-secret clearance, which took months to obtain. . . . The Washington bureaucracy, we discovered, was obsessed about classification. To cite one Orwellian example, Mark Belnick asked the State Department to send a cable for him to the sultan of Brunei, requesting his help in tracing money he had contributed to the Contra cause. Mark drafted the cable and called it in to the State Department, but when he asked the State Department cable operator to read it back to him to make sure the wording was correct, he was told that couldn't be done.
>
> Why not, he asked?
>
> Because, he was told, he didn't have the proper clearance!

Imagine how much greater those sensitivities were with regard to an international tribunal staffed by people from over forty countries. Before the flow of information could begin, many days of discussions and negotiations with relevant officials were required. Conrad Harper played a central role in initiating those discussions. Indeed, I recall his raising this issue with me at our very first meeting. Those discussions culminated in a written agreement between the United States government and the prosecutor. Its complex terms were necessary to provide the assurances required by the United States. That experience made our office a lot more efficient when conducting similar discussions with other governments.

Arthur Liman's story of the cable operator reminded me of a problem that arose regarding the use, as evidence, of photographs Madeleine Albright, then the United States permanent representative at the United Nations, handed to the press during a visit to Bosnia. They were aerial photographs that emerged from evidence given to us by Drazen Erdemović, a former member of the Bosnian Serb Army and the first war criminal to be sentenced by the Yugoslavia tribunal. Ermedović confessed to having murdered more than seventy innocent Muslim men outside Srebrenica in July 1995. His testimony helped verify the occurrence of mass murders in that area, which were later confirmed by Albright's photographs of bodies lying in the vicinity of the grave on the day of the shooting. Photographs taken the following day showed the grave freshly covered with earth. According to a spokesperson for the Bosnian Serb Army, the grave contained the bodies of soldiers killed during battle. Exhumations conducted by the Office of the Prosecutor in the summer of 1996 showed otherwise, however. The persons buried in the grave had been killed by a single gunshot to the back of the head, and most of them had their arms bound behind their backs. The terms of our agreement with the State Department required that we use no such material without their consent. The fact that the material had been made public did not excuse us from having to seek permission. It was not easily obtained. Without our complicated agreement, we could have used the same photographs, which had appeared in any number of newspapers.

This same sensitivity arose in its most exacerbated form in consequence of a letter I addressed to the State Department in 1996. I complained about the unacceptably long time it was taking for my office to receive responses to requests for intelligence information—information that would facilitate our investigations and occasionally help decide whether particular leads should be followed up. On a significant number of occasions we were the recipients of fabricated evidence. We saved much valuable time and expense when we were able to have such information reliably assessed. Attached to my letter was a schedule of coded references to the requests and the dates on which they had been made. To my acute embarrassment, someone in the State Department leaked the letter to the *Washington Post,* which gave it considerable prominence.

The reaction in the State Department, and particularly in the intelligence agencies in Washington, was immediate and explosive. I had no option but to visit Washington in order to attempt to smooth many ruffled feathers. The American media had exacerbated the situation by reporting the matter not as a complaint concerning delay but rather as a complaint that the United States was not providing information it was obliged to give us. The directors of both the Central Intelligence Agency (CIA) and the National Security Council suggested that I should not have committed such matters to writing. I responded by asking whether I should have used open telephone calls for that purpose. There were two consequences of this affair. One was the installation of a safe telephone in my office in The Hague. The second was the immediate expansion of a unit in the CIA specially set up to process requests from the tribunal.

Another matter, which required visits to European capitals, arose from our investigators' need to travel to various countries to seek information and consult with witnesses. I took the view that investigators from the office of an international tribunal should not work in any country without the knowledge and consent of the government of that country. Not to give prior notice would be undiplomatic, especially if a mishap occurred or if government assistance was ultimately required. In practice this concern proved well founded. Most European governments were satisfied with notice through their Dutch embassies. The French government, however, took a formal stance and at first insisted that even willing witnesses could be consulted only through formal court proceedings. That condition proved to be costly and time-consuming. After further representations were made, the French compromised and agreed that unofficial witnesses could be approached informally, but they insisted that any state official, including army personnel, was to be approached only through official channels. Evidence given had to be recorded by an investigating magistrate. Arrangements with the French government entailed a number of visits to Paris.

Another such visit took me to Vienna for meetings with the Austrian government. While there, I decided to respond to the invitation to visit Simon Wiesenthal. Accompanied by Noleen, I was taken to his heavily guarded office in downtown Vienna. That week an octogenarian alleged Nazi war criminal had been sent for trial by a London magistrate. There was considerable public sympathy for the defendant because of his age and the fact that his victims and most of the witnesses were no longer alive. Many were opposed to that kind of trial, some fifty years after the offenses had been committed. I had ambivalent feelings about the prosecution. In the course of a fascinating two-hour discussion, I asked Wiesenthal for his views on the matter. He told us that, from the perspective of the victims, there was really no point to the London prosecution. And from the perspective of the defendant, it was difficult to imagine that after so many years he could be given a fair trial. Nonetheless, he concluded, he fully supported the prosecution. "If you should ever indict Radovan Karadžić, he should know that if he does not face trial, he will be hunted for the rest of his years. That is the only hope of deterring would-be war criminals." Unbeknownst to Wiesenthal, in less than a week I was to announce publicly that we intended to indict

Karadžić and Ratko Mladić, his military commander. At that moment I was convinced that Wiesenthal was correct and, once again, I realized the importance of the tribunal's work.

In October 1994, I visited ministers in Croatia, the Federal Republic of Yugoslavia, and Bosnia. After discussion with my senior colleagues in The Hague, I decided that I should avoid meeting the respective heads of state. In particular, I had no wish to be photographed together with Slobodan Milošević of Serbia or Franjo Tudjman of Croatia, against whom serious criminal allegations had been made and who were the subject of investigations by my office.

Arrangements were made for me to visit the three capitals on this trip, accompanied by senior members of my office. During my time in the Balkans, I learned of the deep sense of victimization the three groups felt, whether actual or perceived, by the other or others. I was given long history lessons in each of the capitals—lessons that did not often merge or have common points of reference. Those visits were important for the amount I was able to learn and understand of the countries where our criminal investigations would be conducted. It seemed to me both before and after the visits that it would have been irresponsible and insulting not to have gone.

Our visit to Sarajevo was unforgettable because of the problems and danger associated with it. During late October, the city of Sarajevo had been under a vicious siege, and the airport had been closed for about two weeks, after the Bosnian Serb Army had fired at United Nations aircraft flying in and out of Sarajevo. The head of the United Nations Protection Force (UNPROFOR) was then Yasushi Akashi, whose office was in Zagreb. Akashi decided to visit Pale to meet with General Mladić in an effort to have the airport reopened. The matter had become urgent, as only one week's supply of food was left in Sarajevo.

Akashi would have to travel to Pale via Sarajevo. A firm supporter of the work of the tribunal, he generously agreed to make room for me and two of my officials, together with General Bertrand de Lapresle, the commander of the United Nations troops, and members of his staff. The plan was to fly from Zagreb to Split along the Dalmatian coast of Croatia in a United Nations airplane—a Russian Yak 30 jet. From Split we were to be taken in two Puma helicopters to Kiseljak, on the border between Croatia and Bosnia. There we were to be met by United Nations vehicles and driven through a number of Serb checkpoints to Sarajevo. We flew to Split and boarded the helicopters. After approximately forty-five minutes we approached Kiseljak and entered thick clouds. Because the airport was not equipped with instrument-landing equipment, it was decided that the mountains in the area made it too dangerous to attempt a landing. There was no option but to return to Split. There Akashi made telephone contact with Mladić. The latter agreed that we should be allowed to fly in helicopters directly to Sarajevo Airport. Mladić instructed his troops in the vicinity of the airport that they were not to fire on or otherwise interfere with our helicopters.

Akashi called me aside and said that he felt that the danger involved in the journey did not justify our joining him. I told him that for a number of reasons I had to insist on proceeding with him. Apart from my need to meet with members of the Bosnian government, investigators from my office were expecting us in Sarajevo. Had I chosen not to go because of this kind of danger, I believed that they would have been justifiably upset. In any event I felt that it was unacceptable for me to send people on my staff to places I would not visit myself. Akashi agreed and we set off.

As we were boarding our helicopter, I remarked to him that I hoped Mladić had efficient means of communicating with his ground troops. He echoed this hope. The captain of the helicopter handed us flak jackets and helmets, which I nervously put on, and I sat down on the uncomfortable seat next to General de Lapresle. Before taking off the captain looked around and told me seriously that I would be well advised not to wear the flack jacket but rather to sit on it. "The bullets," he said, "come from below!"

Toward the end of the tense flight, we flew low over some of the suburbs of Sarajevo. Nothing I had heard, seen, or read about the destruction of the city had prepared me for the actuality: mile after mile of burned-out and destroyed homes. The havoc and misery that humans are capable of inflicting on others continues unabated from century to century. When we landed, the helicopter was immediately surrounded by tanks to protect it from snipers. We alighted in an area surrounded by sandbags.

Akashi went on to Pale, where he would meet Mladić and plead for the reopening of Sarajevo Airport for humanitarian and other United Nations flights. We were driven into Sarajevo for a late lunch with the Bosnian minister of justice. He greeted us cordially and expressed his appreciation of the investigations we had already initiated into ethnic cleansing by the Bosnian Serbs. The quality and quantity of the food and wine, however, struck me as inappropriate in light of the devastation outside the restaurant.

After lunch we went to check in at the Holiday Inn. I recall distinctly the chill in the air—the first sign of the approaching winter. There was fear and apprehension on the faces of the people in the streets. By the time we reached the hotel, it was dusk. There was little illumination, as the only source of electricity was from an emergency generator. One side of the hotel had suffered serious structural damage following direct hits by artillery shells and was heavily boarded. We had to pass that area every time we went to or from our rooms. The atmosphere was gloomy and depressing.

Graham Blewitt and I asked the hotel reception whether it would be possible to call The Hague, where we knew our wives would be anxiously awaiting news of our safe arrival. We were informed that there were no calls out of Sarajevo after 5 o'clock but that we would find a satellite telephone in a room on the first floor. On the door to this room was a large No Smoking sign. I knocked and went in. Through a thick cloud of cigarette smoke, I found a group of young students who explained that they had purchased the satellite dish and telephone to raise funds for an NGO that provided welfare services to the people of Sarajevo. The cost of calls was high and had to be paid in German currency. Graham and I decided that one call to Noleen was sufficient and that she could send a message to Marie Blewitt. I asked one of the students to make the call. The answering machine at our apartment in The Hague was activated, and I recalled that it was an afternoon on which Noleen played bridge. Fortunately we then found Marie Blewitt at home.

After a meager evening snack, we went dejectedly to our rooms. Although there was a television set in my room, I was certain that, with only emergency electricity available, it would not function. I was pleasantly surprised when I pressed the button and it came to life. I could hardly believe that I was watching CNN, which was broadcasting live a joint press conference by Presidents Clinton and Mandela outside the White House. It was a tonic, and after watching the program I fell asleep content that at least in my own country we were on the way to better days.

The flight out of Sarajevo was also fraught with unexpected developments. We had arranged to meet Akashi and his colleagues at Sarajevo Airport early the following afternoon. Akashi arrived a few minutes later than anticipated and informed me that there was a problem. Notwithstanding the agreement he had brokered with Mladić to reopen Sarajevo Airport, the crew of the Russian plane that was supposed to meet us there had refused to fly in. The reason they had given was that they had recently arrived in Zagreb but had never flown to Sarajevo and did not feel confident about the route. Akashi suspected they did not wish to face the danger of being shot at by the Bosnian Serb Army. Alternative arrangements had been made at UNPROFOR headquarters for the Puma helicopters to fly us to Split, where the Yak 30 would be waiting to fly us back to Zagreb.

Akashi, however, was determined not to fly out of Sarajevo in a helicopter. He had negotiated with Mladić for fixed-wing aircraft to fly into and out of Sarajevo, and he felt it important for the morale of the people of Sarajevo and for the credibility of his mission that he be seen leaving in a fixed-wing aircraft. He had arranged for a United Nations Russian Antonov troop carrier to fly from Zagreb with the first supplies for Sarajevo. It would not be arriving until some hours later, and we would have to wait for it. I agreed with Akashi's rationale and I told him so.

Not more than a few minutes later, a messenger informed Akashi that the badly mutilated bodies of some Muslim soldiers had been discovered in the hills behind Sarajevo. Akashi was extremely concerned at the fury this news would cause and worried that it would further exacerbate the already tense situation in Bosnia. He decided that he should personally investigate the allegations and thereupon left for the headquarters of General Sir Michael Rose, commander of the United Nations troops in Bosnia. Akashi was away for many long hours, during which the Antonov arrived, ready to take us back to Zagreb. When he returned, we learned that the bodies had in fact not been mutilated but had suffered the ravages of the early snow. It was a slow, cold, and depressing return trip on the uncomfortable Antonov.

That visit to the former Yugoslavia was the start of cooperation between the Bosnian and Croatian authorities and the Office of the Prosecutor. Without personal contact with the relevant players, such cooperation would not have been possible. In particular I built a friendly relationship with Ivan Simonović, who was then the Croatian deputy minister of foreign affairs and formerly the dean of the law school at the University of Zagreb. That we were both lawyers and wine lovers certainly helped. Another friendship that developed was with Muhamed Sacirbey. When I became the chief prosecutor, Sacirbey was the permanent representative of Bosnia and Herzegovina to the United Nations. On one of my early visits to New York, he invited me to have lunch with him in the Delegates' Dining Room at the U.N. His support for the work of the tribunal was consistent. Subsequently, Sacirbey became the minister of foreign affairs. I did not have the opportunity of building personal relationships with anyone from Belgrade because of the extreme antagonism toward, and suspicion of, the tribunal on the Serb side.

In the first months after I took up my office in The Hague, additional matters took me to several European capitals as well as to Washington, D.C., and Ottawa. The trips to Washington served a number of purposes. Apart from garnering support from the United States administration and Congress, we had received important offers from law schools to assist with research on many of our difficult problems. At that time we did not have a law library at our offices in The Hague. Plus, in those days our legal section was understaffed. Professor Diane Orentlicher, of the American University Law School in Washington, was particularly generous with her time. On one occasion I requested an urgent opinion from her on a difficult issue relating to the effect on subsequent proceedings of trials in absentia. My request could not have come at a worse time for her—she was in the middle of final examinations. That did not deter her, however, and within a few days I had a well-researched opinion covering the law in a number of relevant jurisdictions around the world.

In about March or April 1995 I found it necessary to justify my travels and thus to assert my independence. At a difficult meeting with the secretary-general in New York, he berated me for being outside The Hague so frequently. My relationship with the secretary-general and with the senior members of his Secretariat was complex and often troubled. Part of the difficulty lay in the fact that the Security Countil had created the Office of Chief Prosecutor expressly as an independent unit. I do not know of any other officials of the United Nations who have this independence other than the judges of the International Court of Justice and the two War Crimes Tribunals. In this regard, my position was not comparable to that of judges who seldom came into contact with the United Nations Secretariat.

My contact with Boutros-Ghali revealed a mercurial personality. I met with him on four occasions, and on all but one we were alone. We had two major differences. The first related to my travels outside The Hague on official business. In his view, I should have been spending all my time in my office "researching the law of war crimes and directing the investigations." He was not impressed with my explanation that we needed the cooperation of the governments involved to proceed successfully with our investigations. Also, in order to ensure that cooperation, I had no option but to make personal contact with relevant government ministers and senior administration officials. I was astounded when he told me that if I needed to speak to political leaders I should request them to come and see me. He said that was his practice! I responded that it was impractical for me to operate in that fashion. I was surprised and annoyed to discover that the secretary-general had requested the Registrar's Office at the tribunal to furnish him with full details of my travels. He had the statistics and knew precisely what trips I had made and how many days I had been away. Boutros-Ghali also informed me that some of the permanent representatives at the United Nations had complained that I spent too much time with Americans, and he agreed with these sentiments. I informed him that I disagreed with his general approach but that I would take into account his concerns about frequent visits to Washington. My attitude made it quite clear to the secretary-general that I did not intend to change my policy.

The Security Council had indeed been prudent when, in the statute for the tribunal, the independence of the chief prosecutor was unambiguously guaranteed. That guarantee was crucial to my relationship with Boutros-Ghali, as indeed with other senior members of the United Nations Secretariat.

An even more important and difficult area of my relationship with the tribunal judges and the secretary-general concerned the question of prosecutorial discretion and policy. It arose most acutely with the indictment of Karadžić and Mladić. The first public notice of possible indictments against them was my announcement that I intended to seek an order from the tribunal requesting that the government of Bosnia and Herzegovina defer their investigations against these two war criminals to those of my office. But before making that announcement, I required a date of hearing from the president of the tribunal. It was not my intention to discuss the merits of the deferral application with the tribunal president—that would have been both unnecessary and inappropriate. Whether the application was well founded would be for a trial chamber of three judges to decide. Antonio Cassese, however, offered the strongest objection to my proposal for such an order. I should present a proper indictment or nothing, he claimed. He was not aware of the state of our investigation or of the reasons why we first wished to have a deferral order. Had I briefed Cassese on the information in our possession, that might well have made it impossible for him to have sat in an appeal relating to an indictment of Karadžić and Mladić. Our disagreement over this matter was serious, and for some weeks there was all but a rupture between my office and the judges' chambers. I nonetheless persisted in moving for the application. The Bosnian government not only acquiesced, it welcomed it. The application was granted by the trial chamber, enabling us to obtain further information from the Bosnian authorities in Sarajevo. The first indictment against Karadžić and Mladić soon followed, on charges that included genocide and crimes against humanity. As in the situation with the secretary-general, my independence relative to the judges was crucial to the performance of my duties.

The indictments and warrants of arrest against Karadžić and Mladić led to another difficult exchange with the secretary-general. Prudence dictated that I warn a number of officials of the impending deferral application. One was Akashi, who, as the special representative of the secretary-general, had overall control of the United Nations Mission in the former Yugoslavia. Others were Sadaka Ogata, United Nations High Commissioner for Refugees, and Cornelio Sommaruga, president of the International Committee of the Red Cross. The High Commission for Refugees and the International Committee of the Red Cross had a substantial number of aid workers and representatives in the former Yugoslavia, and I felt certain they would want to take special precautions ahead of the announcement. The United Nations troops and aid workers could have been in danger if the Bosnian Serbs had decided to take hostages or other retaliatory action. In the case of United Nations personnel, I felt that some Serbs would not make neat distinctions between different agencies of the United Nations. At my request, Akashi agreed to meet me in Geneva, and in the strictest confidence I gave him advance warning of my action. He felt compelled to pass this information to Boutros-Ghali, and I had no objection to his doing so.

A few months later, soon after the indictments had been issued, I met with the secretary-general. He started by remarking that he was surprised the tribunal had indicted Karadžić without consulting him and without seeking his views on the matter. Taken aback, I replied that on no account would I have consulted him. In any event, I reminded him, he had been aware even before the deferral application that an indictment against Karadžić was in the pipeline—a point he conceded. But he would not have approached me, he added, as that would have been inconsistent with my independence, which he fully respected. I realized then that he would not have regarded consultation with him on the indictment as inconsistent with that independence. He made it clear that had I consulted him, he would have advised me not to indict Karadžić before peace had been brokered in Bosnia. I was relieved that Boutros-Ghali had not attempted to intervene in the matter, though he must have been sorely tempted.

The political assessment of Boutros-Ghali over the timing of the indictment of Karadžić turned out to be incorrect. Had he not been indicted, the Dayton Accords would not have been brokered. Karadžić would have been free to attend the meetings, and that would have made the attendance of Alija Izetbegović, the president of Bosnia, impossible. It must be remembered that the Dayton meetings took place no more than four months after the massacre of Muslim men and boys outside Srebrenica. Some months after Dayton, during an address in New York, I referred to this matter. To my surprise Sacirbey was in the audience and confirmed that President Izetbegović would not have considered attending any meeting at which Karadžić was present.

Early in 1996 I had a further meeting with Boutros-Ghali, during which I expressed my frustration at the refusal of troops of the North Atlantic Treaty Organization (NATO) to arrest indicted alleged war criminals. The secretary-general again voiced his disquiet at the decision to indict Karadžić and Mladić while the war was still being fought. He added, however, that once they had been indicted and warrants for their arrest had been issued, he had no doubt that the members of the United Nations had a duty to see that they were arrested and delivered for trial in The Hague.

I also decided that I would give prior notice of proceedings against Karadžić and Mladić to Hans van Mierlo, the Dutch foreign minister. Within hours I was requested to brief the ministers of foreign affairs, justice, and defense. As a consequence, the security of important government buildings in The Hague and Amsterdam was increased. Also within hours, I had a visit from the head of the Royal and Diplomatic Protection Unit, who informed me that I was to have round-the-clock protection. This meant that while in the Netherlands I would travel accompanied by two armed bodyguards in an armored motorcar; two other bodyguards in a second vehicle would proceed to my intended destinations some minutes ahead of my arrival. Within hours a mobile police post was erected outside our apartment building, much to the interest of the people who lived there. Police officers manned the post day and night.

Eventually, these guards were replaced by video cameras connected to monitors in a nearby police station. My confidence in this system was dented some months after it began, however. As part of a major refurbishing of the apartment building, scaffolding had been erected across the facade. One of our neighbors was at home one evening and saw a young man scampering past her window. Looking out, she found two youngsters freely climbing up and down the scaffolding. Their activity elicited no response from the police. The Protection Unit, on the other hand, was impressive. The concern with which its members approached their work was exceptional. Of course, it was ironic that one of the reasons Noleen had had for leaving South Africa the previous July was to escape the intrusion of security concerns. Here they were again, with a vengeance.

One might ask whether and to what extent the independence of the tribunal was compromised by its reliance on the General Assembly for finances. Soon after I arrived at The Hague I was informed that no budget as yet existed for the tribunal and that the budget committee of the United Nations would have to approve one. The Advisory Committee on Administrative and Budgetary Questions, known by the acronym ACABQ, is made up of representatives elected by the General Assembly and vets expenditures of each committee and agency of the organization. Once appointed, the representatives become independent of the governments that nominated them.

It was the responsibility of the registrar of the tribunal and me to justify our budget proposal before the ACABQ. Those knowledgeable in U.N. affairs advised me that it was a most unpleasant experience; that every item of our draft budget would be examined in detail and that many of the members were difficult if not unpleasant. My first appearance, in December 1994, was preceded by much preparation. I asked Graham Blewitt to accompany me, as he was primarily responsible for the setup of the office and had a far better grasp of the details than I. After all the warnings we had received, we were pleasantly surprised that the hearings of the ACABQ turned out to be both enjoyable and interesting. The members were fascinated with the idea of a war crimes tribunal, and much of the time was spent discussing the general philosophy of humanitarian law and the policies we would be pursuing in the Office of the Prosecutor. Generally speaking, that committee was generous in the amounts it recommended for the budget of both the Yugoslavia and Rwanda tribunals. Its chairperson for more than two decades, Ambassador Conrad Mselle of Uganda, was particularly interested, especially when the Rwanda tribunal was established in November 1994.

There was one unfortunate aspect related to the first budget meeting. I had also been informed ahead of time that at least one indictment had to be issued before the November meeting in order to demonstrate that the system was working and that the tribunal was worthy of financial support. It must be remembered that the United Nations was already then starved for cash and that every dollar voted for the tribunal was one dollar less for other important agencies. For that reason we issued our first indictment, against Dragan Nicolić, who, despite the despicable nature of his alleged conduct, was a comparatively low-level member of the Bosnian Serb forces. At that time he was the only person against whom we had sufficient evidence to justify an indictment for war crimes, but he was hardly an appropriate defendant for the first indictment issued by the first ever international war crimes tribunal.

Mselle was particularly understanding when it appeared that the opening of the Constitutional Court of South Africa on 15 February 1995 would clash with the adjourned hearing of the ACABQ on the tribunal's budget. It was obviously desirable that all eleven justices of South Africa's new court attend and take their oaths of office in the presence of President Mandela. Mselle felt strongly that the opening ceremony for the Constitutional Court took precedence over the work of the ACABQ. He therefore rearranged its schedule to accommodate me.

The ceremony in Johannesburg was memorable. I shall never forget the opening words of Mandela. He recalled that the last time he had been in a South African court was in 1963, when he was awaiting a possible death sentence. His words were particularly poignant, because the following day the first appeal related to the constitutionality of the death sentence in light of the Bill of Rights, which formed part of the interim Constitution. As I had to return immediately to The Hague, I did not participate in the hearing or decision of that case, but my colleagues unanimously held that the death sentence was unconstitutional. No executions have taken place in South Africa since the de Klerk government put them on hold in 1989.

The media played an important role in ensuring an adequate level of political and financial support for the tribunal. When I arrived at The Hague, the publicity could not have been more negative, which was hardly surprising given the length of time taken to appoint a chief prosecutor. To my mind, if we were to succeed it was essential to have media support. Fortunately the tribunal had already enlisted Christian Chartier as its media spokesperson. Chartier was highly experienced with the media, having worked for some years for a leading Paris newspaper. He was my constant adviser and invariably pointed me in the correct direction. His rich Gallic humor is perhaps his most endearing characteristic. The strong support the tribunal received from the written and electronic media in many countries, much of it due to Chartier, made a substantial difference to its fortunes.

Of course, media attention has its downside. Before the indictment of Karadžić and Mladić, reporters were critical because of the "small fish" we had indicted. Then after Karadžić and Mladić, the question I was asked almost daily was when were we going to indict President Milošević. For some years there had been widespread speculation in political and media circles that Milošević, more than any other leader in the region, was behind the criminal policies of the Bosnian Serb Army. After some months the charge was made that I had been pressured by the major powers not to indict Milošević. What the media did not appear to recognize was that making war is not a war crime. Waging an aggressive war is certainly recognized as a crime by international law, but it is not a crime within the jurisdiction of the tribunal. That Milošević may have approved of the criminal conduct of Karadžić and Mladić did not make him guilty of a war crime. Nor did the fact that he supplied weapons or even troops to the Bosnian Serb Army. To indict Milošević it was necessary to establish before a criminal tribunal that he was a party to the crimes committed by the Bosnian Serb Army. Had there been such evidence he would have been indicted. I frequently assured the public that no person ever pressed me to refrain from indicting Milošević or anyone else. Indeed, had such pressure been applied I would instantaneously have made it public.

Similar allegations were made when Karadžić and Mladić were indicted for the second time for the war crimes committed in July 1995, when the Bosnian Serbs invaded and took control of Srebrenica. That indictment was issued during the Dayton negotiations, which resulted in the agreement that put a stop to the fighting. There was wide speculation that the timing of the indictment was not a coincidence and that it was used to pressure the negotiators to take account of the interests of the tribunal. In fact the investigation of war crimes in Srebrenica had started some weeks before there was any suggestion of the Dayton negotiations. We gave preference to that investigation because of persistent stories of the massacre of thousands of Muslim men and boys by the Bosnian Serb Army, led by Mladić. When it was announced that the Dayton talks were to take place, we decided to hasten the indictment. That we succeeded in issuing it when we did remained a coincidence.

In parenthesis, it must be remembered that the process of issuing an indictment is highly complex. The investigation leading to an indictment is conducted by one of the teams in the prosecutor's office. When that team has completed its work, an indictment is drafted, usually with the assistance of one of the senior trial lawyers. It is then submitted for careful scrutiny to a meeting of all the lawyers in the office. With all relevant documents and witness statements in hand, they check the draft word for word and satisfy themselves that the charges are appropriate and sufficiently supported by the evidence. That process may last days or even weeks. Only when these lawyers are satisfied is it submitted for final approval to the chief prosecutor and the deputy prosecutor. At that point further questions were invariably raised by Blewitt and me, and on occasion further investigations were requested.

After the chief prosecutor signs the indictment, it is submitted to one of the trial judges for confirmation. That judge usually calls in the chief prosecutor and requests further information; not infrequently the merits of the indictments or aspects of it are debated. That review process might take days or even weeks.

Anyone understanding this process would appreciate how impossible it would be to have an indictment coincide with a three-week-long meeting. In any event, had the indictment been issued before Dayton, we would doubtless have been accused of trying to influence the outcome of the meeting; had we issued it after the agreement, the allegation would have been that we were pressured to delay it so as not to interfere with the outcome.

On the night of 6 April 1994 the gruesome genocide began in Rwanda. In a period of less than two hundred days, between five hundred thousand and one million Rwandans were murdered by their fellow citizens. The efficiency of the killings surprised the international community. Later that year, the Tutsi-led army, under the command of Paul Kagami, drove the organizers and supporters of the genocide into the former Zaire. A new government under President Pasteur Bizimungu took control, with Kagami as deputy president.

At that time Rwanda held one of the nonpermanent seats on the Security Council. Their representative requested that the United Nations establish an international criminal tribunal to investigate, try, and punish those responsible for the killings. The criminal justice system within Rwanda had been practically wiped out. Over 90 percent of the judges and prosecutors, mostly Hutu, had been murdered (moderate Hutus who opposed the genocide were also targeted by Hutu extremists). With the Yugoslavia tribunal as precedent, the Security Council had no difficulty in agreeing to the request and prepared a statute for the United Nations Criminal Tribunal for Rwanda. When members of the Rwandan government read the terms of the statute, they changed their minds and informed the Security Council that they no longer wished to have a tribunal. However, the diplomatic and bureaucratic machinery having been activated, there was no way to stop it, and the Security Council insisted on proceeding. When the resolution was put to the vote toward the end of November 1994, thirteen members voted in favor and only one, Rwanda, voted against the resolution. China, having some sympathy for the position of Rwanda, abstained from voting.

The Security Council decided that the chief prosecutor of the Yugoslavia tribunal should assume that post for the Rwanda tribunal as well. The seat of the tribunal would be Arusha, in northern Tanzania. It was believed, justifiably, that no fair trials could have been held in the presence of millions of victims calling for blood. The security of both defense lawyers and judges would have been virtually impossible to maintain. To placate the feelings of the Rwandan government, however, the Security Council decreed that the Office of the Prosecutor be set up in Kigali, the capital of Rwanda. The council also instructed the Office of Legal Affairs to take responsibility for the establishment of the Rwanda tribunal.

I was thus given the task of creating a new office in Rwanda. Because of the negative vote of Rwanda in the Security Council, I decided to visit Kigali as soon as possible and open discussions with the government of Rwanda. Accordingly I called the Office of Legal Affairs and informed the director, Ralph Zacklin, of my intention to visit Rwanda. He replied that before my visit, officials of the United Nations from New York (including Zacklin) should open discussions in Kigali. I had no objection, on the condition that they take place in the immediate future. A week later, at the end of the first week of December, when I called Zacklin to ask about plans, he said there was no hurry. I disagreed and told him that I was determined to visit Kigali before Christmas and would make arrangements to go there the following week. Zacklin then asked where I intended finding the money for my proposed trip, since no start-up funds had yet been appropriated for the Rwanda tribunal and at that time there were no funds in the special trust fund that had been set up by the secretary-general. I asked if I could raise the funds, but his response was noncommittal. As it happened, on the following day I had an appointment to discuss the Yugoslavia tribunal with Flavio Cotti, the foreign minister of Switzerland. During the course of our discussion, Minister Cotti (who in 1998 assumed the presidency of the Swiss Confederation) asked me about the Rwanda tribunal, and I repeated my conversation with Zacklin. Cotti immediately turned to his assistant and instructed him to deposit one hundred thousand Swiss francs in the Special Trust Fund for Rwanda that same day. Now I had the funds to travel to Rwanda, he remarked with a smile. When I later informed Zacklin, he sounded unhappy and said that it was not appropriate for officials of the United Nations to raise funds from governments. I consoled myself with the thought that Switzerland was not a member of the United Nations! In any event, that is how I was able to pay for my first visit to Kigali.

That visit proved to be an important one. I learned that Rwanda had three objections to the tribunal, as established. The first was that its seat was not in Kigali and that the trials would be held in a foreign, albeit neighboring, country. In its request for an international tribunal, the Rwandan government had intended, through a speedy international effort, to bring the criminal leaders to justice in Rwanda. Secondly, they objected to the fact that the tribunal would not have the power to order the execution of any defendant brought before it.

As President Bizimungu explained to me during that first visit, a few months after so many of his people had been slaughtered was hardly an appropriate time to suggest the abolition of the death penalty— even if he himself was an abolitionist. He also pointed out that because convicted defendants would certainly be sentenced to death when the Rwandan courts were reconstituted, the treatment of those accused of crimes relating to the genocide would be uneven. The most guilty criminals would be brought before the international tribunal, have their rights protected by counsel, and, if convicted, be sentenced to life imprisonment in a comfortable United Nations–supervised prison. Those who were probably less guilty would be tried in less efficient courts in Rwanda and sentenced to death. At the same time the president recognized that in 1994 the international community would not be prepared to establish a criminal tribunal with the power to impose the death sentence. Certainly the nations of western Europe would not have countenanced it. The third objection was that the temporal jurisdiction of the tribunal was limited to the calendar year of 1994. The government was convinced that the planning of the genocide began in 1992 and 1993. On this score I was able to reassure President Bizimungu that if the crimes were committed during 1994, I had no doubt that we could indict persons regardless of when they planned the commission of the crimes. His fears over the exclusion of the death penalty became a reality when, during 1998, the Rwandan government executed less-guilty persons while the tribunal was sentencing the real leaders to life imprisonment. There was really no way to resolve this problem.

Notwithstanding the serious concerns of the Rwandan government over the United Nations tribunal, from that first visit I developed a cordial relationship with the Rwandan leaders. At all times they cooperated in setting up an office in Kigali and assisted our investigators in doing their work. That cooperation survived some difficult meetings when, on behalf of the tribunal, I considered it my duty to insist that the primacy of the tribunal be respected. Those difficulties reached a climax when the Rwandan government demanded that I withdraw a request to the Cameroons to have Colonel Theoneste Bagasora transferred for trial to Arusha. Bagasora was the alleged leader of the genocide, and the government was determined that he should stand trial and face execution in Kigali. Unwilling to compromise, I said I would prefer the tribunal to cease its activities rather than defer to the national courts of Rwanda. At that time there were no courts operating in Rwanda, and it was many months later that national trials began. Tens of thousands of suspects were being held in the worst imaginable prison conditions, and I was convinced that Bagasora had little chance of surviving to stand trial if he was transferred to Rwanda at that time. And, most important, if an international tribunal with primacy of jurisdiction had been established by the Security Council, it would have been inappropriate for the arch criminal not to be tried before that tribunal.

In December 1994, when I first visited Rwanda, Kigali was still in a state of ruination. Schools and shops were closed, and there were few people on the streets. Many Rwandans had strong feelings against the United Nations because of its regrettable failure to prevent or stop the genocide that previous April. Fortunately for me, the secretary-general had appointed as his representative in Rwanda a consummate diplomat, Shahryar Khan, a former Pakistani High Commissioner in London. Without the advice and assistance of Khan my difficult task would have been infinitely more intractable. He insisted that during that first visit I stay at the Belgian Village, a well-secured military compound that housed the United Nations troops. Between December 1994 and my departure from office at the end of September 1996, I paid fourteen visits to Rwanda, two of which were spent as Khan's houseguest. One of the privileges of my work was the opportunity to spend time with Khan. Apart from his intellectual and diplomatic skills, I also admired his physical fitness—he is an avid squash and tennis player.

Some people have regarded the Rwanda tribunal as some sort of poor relation of the Yugoslavia tribunal. That perception is quite unjustified. Financially the two tribunals were treated equally. Indeed, the secretary-general was, if anything, better disposed to the former than to the latter. Apart from his own African roots, Boutros-Ghali had been outspokenly critical of the manner in which the international community had left Rwanda in the lurch in its most desperate hour. And that was true also of the budget committee of the United Nations. The problems that arose had nothing to do with any form of discrimination against the Rwanda tribunal. The initial difficulty was finding sufficient funds to establish the tribunal before a budget was approved by the United Nations. The second was finding suitably qualified personnel to work in Kigali. Because of the difficult security situation, spouses were not allowed to join those appointed to posts there. For the first couple of years all members of my office had no option but to stay in one of two hotels in the city. There was no form of recreation or other diversion available, which meant that the personnel were living together during all their waking hours. The hotel became an extension of their offices. The atmosphere was not congenial. Yet another difficulty was achieving gender balance within the staff. What was already a challenge in The Hague, in an office dominated by investigators, became even more so in Kigali.

Jan Pronk, the Dutch minister of development aid, played a major role in raising the start-up funds. The generosity of his government was quite out of the ordinary. Holland's provision of personnel, equipment, and funds for the Rwanda tribunal was second only to the United States'. At a time when we were struggling for funds, Pronk conceived of the idea of holding an international funding meeting in Kigali. He suggested that, in my capacity as chief prosecutor, I convene the meeting, which was enthusiastically supported by John Shattuck, the United States deputy assistant secretary of state for human rights. I agreed to do so, notwithstanding a lukewarm response from the United Nations Secretariat. The meeting was held and the result was well beyond our expectations. Funds in excess of $6 million were pledged.

During 1996 a new problem emerged with the announced pullout of the United Nations from Rwanda. The U.N. troops had guaranteed the physical safety of my staff in Kigali. I first heard the news from a United Nations driver who used to meet me at Nairobi airport when I stopped over there en route to Kigali. I could not imagine that he would receive such information before I did and therefore assumed there was no substance in his report. When I arrived in Kigali, however, I met with General Jean-Claude Toussignant, the commander of the United Nations troops. To my amazement he confirmed the report. Only after many meetings in Kigali and New York and many press reports about the people working in Rwanda did the United Nations Secretariat make adequate security arrangements. During that period I seriously contemplated having to close the office in Kigali.

Apart from sharing a chief prosecutor, the Rwanda and Yugoslavia tribunals also shared an appeals chamber of five judges. Accordingly it was necessary for the United Nations to appoint only six trial judges for the Rwanda tribunal. I was delighted when I heard that one of them was a fellow South African, Judge Navanathem Pillay, from Durban. I have received many reports of the sterling work performed by her in Arusha. In particular she has given attention to gender-related offenses and to the concerns of female victims and witnesses. She has also been an effective spokesperson for international justice. I was delighted when in June 1999 she became the president of the tribunal.

The work of the two tribunals and the conditions in which they operate are so different that comparisons are meaningless. Both share the disadvantage of working at a distance from the site of the crimes it is their duty to prosecute. In both Arusha and The Hague, however, the two tribunals have demonstrated that they are able to hold fair and just trials consistent with the highest international standards. As their work progresses, I remain optimistic that the painstaking manner in which they have been recording the sordid history of their respective areas of jurisdiction will benefit the victims of the former Yugoslavia and Rwanda, respectively.

Much time during my last months in office as chief prosecutor was spent in pushing the North Atlantic Command to order NATO troops to arrest the alleged war criminals we had indicted in the former Yugo-slavia. In particular, I had in mind Karadžić and Mladić. From the infor-mation at my disposal it was clear that the stumbling block was the Pen-tagon. (Richard Holbrooke has since confirmed that in his account of the Dayton negotiations.) [5] With the assistance of David Scheffer, I was able to discuss this issue with William Perry, the secretary for defense; Anthony Lake, the president's security adviser; and John Deutch, the director of the CIA. All of them were frank in conceding that the United States military was strongly opposed to a robust policy on arrests. Perry informed me that the Pentagon was concerned not so much with deaths or injuries in the course of arrests but with possible reprisals after the arrests. I argued strongly that the international community, with the leadership of the United States, had undertaken, through the Security Council, to bring justice to the hundreds of thousands of victims in Bosnia. I pointed out that tens of thousands of the best-equipped troops in the world were in Bosnia and that the victims were unable to under-stand how the war criminals responsible for their misery were allowed to strut about in freedom under the noses of the soldiers. I also passed on the messages of frustration that had been relayed to our investiga-tors in Bosnia by a number of senior members of the United States and British armies who would have welcomed orders to arrest the indicted war criminals.

I deeply regret that the political leaders of the United States were not prepared to go against the will of their military leadership. The history of post-Dayton Bosnia could have been very different if Karadžić and Mladić had been brought to trial in The Hague. There is the likelihood that solid evidence would have emerged of the role played by Milošević and his government in the ethnic cleansing in Bosnia. And, conceiv-ably, the subsequent ethnic cleansing in Kosovo in 1999 might have been avoided.

It should be added that the European members of NATO offered little support for a strong policy on arrests. An exception was Klaus Kinkel, the German foreign minister, who at all times, both privately and publicly, called for arrests. During 1997 and 1998 a more positive approach was adopted with the support of Robin Cook, when he became the British foreign minister, and Madeleine Albright, when she became U.S. secretary of state.

When my leave of absence from the South African Constitutional Court was granted, it was intended that I should return to South Africa at the end of July 1996. As events turned out, my return to the court had become necessary in light of an unusual task which fell on that Court at that time—the certification process for South Africa's new Constitution. That Constitution was to be drafted by a constitutional assembly consisting of the members of both houses of the new, democratically elected Parliament. However, the interim Constitution provided that the new constitutional text had to comply with thirty-four constitutional principles contained in a schedule to the interim Constitution. It was provided further that the new text would be of no force or effect unless the Constitutional Court certified that the provisions of the new text complied with the constitutional principles. This was a procedure without any precedent. In effect it called upon the Constitutional Court to test the constitutionality of the Constitution. The process was obviously of the highest political moment, and all relevant role players believed that the Court as originally constituted should sit on the matter.

Early in 1996 it had been agreed that NATO forces would remain in Bosnia until the end of that year. The United States administration took the view that a new chief prosecutor should not be installed in The Hague until that time. Warren Christopher, then secretary of state, requested that I remain in my post for an additional six months. I indicated to him that I was happy to do so but that the decision would rest with President Mandela and the South African government. President

Clinton sent a letter to Mandela requesting his agreement to an extension of my term of office. In his response, Mandela noted that my return to the court was considered urgent and expressed his reluctance to accede to the extension. After a further exchange of letters between the two presidents it was agreed that I would remain in The Hague for an additional three months, until the end of September 1996, on condition that I would be available to sit with my colleagues in the constitutional certification process. During June and July 1996 I returned to South Africa for three weeks and participated in the interesting and complex court proceedings. In the end the court was unanimous in withholding its certification, and the constitutional assembly had to be recalled to amend the text in light of the court's opinion. In a subsequent hearing, the Constitution was certified and came into force in February 1997.

There was much press comment when I left office as chief prosecutor. Some journalists were keen to report that I was leaving because of my frustration at the refusal of NATO to order the arrest of war criminals indicted by the tribunal. Others wished to ascribe my departure to frustration with U.N. inefficiency. These would have been stories worth reporting. With the help of Christian Chartier, however, I was successful in convincing the reporters of the actual reasons for my return to South Africa. It helped that my original appointment, announced in July 1994, was expressly stated to be for a two-year period.

My term of office as chief prosecutor ended on a particularly high note. U.S. Supreme Court Justice Sandra Day O'Connor heads the board of the Central and Eastern Europe Law Initiative of the American Bar Association (CEELI), which had generously supported the work of the tribunals. Indeed, without the support of CEELI, the first defendant, Dusan Tadić, would not have had a fair trial. At his request the tribunal had appointed a leading Dutch criminal attorney, Michael Vladimiroff, to defend him. The procedure used in the tribunals allows for cross-examination of witnesses, a practice foreign to the inquisitorial systems adopted by many countries in western Europe, including the Netherlands. When the director of CEELI, Mark Ellis, approached me soon after my appointment as chief prosecutor, he inquired as to how CEELI could assist my office. I suggested that the most important form of assistance would be to ensure that defendants were adequately represented. Ellis agreed, and CEELI briefed and paid the fees of two members of the London Bar to assist the Dutch lawyer and to conduct the cross-examination of the prosecution witnesses. At the beginning of October 1996, Justice O'Connor hosted a memorable dinner in my honor in the Great Hall of the United States Supreme Court. Both she and Madeleine Albright spoke in support of the work of the tribunals and were generous in their praise for the achievements during my tenure.

Toward an International Criminal Court

Since World War II, humanitarian and human rights lawyers have been calling for the establishment of a permanent international criminal court. In the first United Nations human rights convention, the Genocide Convention, there is reference to such a court. Unfortunately, in my opinion, the major nations of the world viewed this idea as a threat to national sovereignty: they did not wish an international tribunal to sit in judgment over their own citizens. As discussed in Chapter 4, it was the horror of ethnic cleansing in Europe in the early 1990s that led the Security Council to set up the Yugoslavia tribunal. With that precedent, it was not surprising that the council established a second international tribunal to bring the perpetrators to justice.

The two United Nations tribunals provided a new impetus to the movement for an international criminal court. However, even the most optimistic supporters of a permanent court did not anticipate that before the turn of the century a diplomatic conference would be called to consider a treaty, let alone that such a treaty would be approved by 120 members of the United Nations.

Although human rights activists are understandably impatient to have such a court established, they tend to overlook the tremendous advances that have been made since World War II in creating a universal criminal jurisdiction for war crimes. This advance was dramatically demonstrated at the end of 1998 during the proceedings in London against General Augusto Pinochet, the former military dictator of Chile. A few years ago the idea of a former dictator being arrested in England at the insistence of a Spanish judge for crimes committed years earlier in Chile would have been regarded as fanciful. Whether the proceedings were permissible against a former head of state depended upon the interpretation of the British legislation that controls extradition and, in particular, upon the reach of the doctrine of sovereign immunity. That domestic legal issue in no way detracted from the British courts' acceptance of the principle that Spain's claim was in all other respects a proper one. Indeed, there were competing claims to extradite Pinochet from seven other European nations.

The principal objection from Chile was that Pinochet should be tried before their own courts for alleged human rights abuses. In theory that might be so, but the fact is that Pinochet was effectively granted an amnesty in return for allowing democratic elections and for handing over power to the head of the elected government, President Aylwin. At age eighty-three there is no prospect of a serious prosecution against Pinochet in his home country.

The Pinochet affair throws into stark relief the tensions between prosecutions and amnesties and demonstrates the necessity for a permanent international criminal court. Would an apartheid criminal who has been granted an amnesty by the Truth and Reconciliation Commission be liable to be prosecuted for crimes against humanity in a non–South African court? Would South Africa be obliged, on a request from Britain, to extradite the bombers of the ANC headquarters in London if they have been granted an amnesty by the Truth and Reconciliation Commission? Should a distinction be made between apartheid crimes committed in South Africa and those committed in cross-border raids in Botswana or Swaziland? These are complex issues whose resolution is neither obvious nor easy.

Problems such as these will clearly face the prosecutor of a permanent international criminal court. I have no doubt that such a prosecutor should not be inhibited by national amnesties. In international law they clearly have no standing and would not afford a defense to criminal or civil proceedings before an international court or a national court other than that of the country which grants the amnesty. That does not mean that in deciding on an investigation or prosecution, the prosecutor will not take into account amnesty processes. Where states take upon themselves the task of addressing their past, international observers must consider the motives impelling them to do so. Societies in transition often choose to forgo systematic prosecutions for fear of destabilizing the new democracy. Nevertheless I would suggest that an international prosecutor ignore self-amnesties of the kind granted to General Pinochet. On the other hand, in South Africa amnesties have been granted by the Truth and Reconciliation Commission in consequence of legislation approved by a democratically elected legislature — a legislature that is representative of the victims of apartheid. It would be appropriate for an international prosecutor to consider the wishes of such victims and to take into account the moral justification for amnesty proceedings and whether in the context it enables the society (as it did in South Africa) to end repression in a relatively peaceful manner.

The essence of justice is its universality, both nationally and internationally. A decent and rational person is offended that criminal laws should apply only to some people and not to others in similar situations. I felt distinctly uncomfortable when, in October 1994, in Belgrade, I was asked by the Serb minister of justice why the United Nations had established a War Crimes Tribunal for the former Yugoslavia when it had not done so for Cambodia or Iraq. Why were the people of the former Yugoslavia being treated differently? Was this an act of discrimination? The only answer I could give was that the international community had to begin somewhere, but that if there was no follow-through and if other equivalent situations in the future were not treated comparably, then the people of the former Yugoslavia could justifiably claim discrimination.

It is important to have regard for the successes of the United Nations tribunals. The most significant is the acceptance today that an international court is able to dispense justice—that a fair trial before such a tribunal is possible. Many serious and well-intentioned experts and commentators doubted that judges from five continents, sitting together, could conduct criminal trials that would be judged fair by international standards. Others doubted that there could be fair and successful international investigations and prosecutions. That was the challenge given to the judges and prosecutors in The Hague and in Arusha. At all times, in the Office of the Prosecutor, the primary goal was not to achieve convictions but rather to ensure that those indicted would enjoy fair processes and procedures. That goal was by and large achieved.

The second success of the United Nations tribunals has been a tremendous advance of international humanitarian law and international procedural law—a natural product of the law being turned to practical effect. For over a century, humanitarian law (what used to be called the law of war) has been the subject of international conferences and has been of interest to academic lawyers. Prior to 1993 it was hardly ever used or tested in courts of law. In those circumstances the sophistication and coherence of humanitarian law is a commendable achievement, the credit for which must unreservedly go to the International Committee of the Red Cross (ICRC). The first Geneva Convention was the outcome of a diplomatic conference called by the ICRC in 1864. The substantial advances in humanitarian law since then have been the legacy to future generations from this organization, which has always been regarded as the guardian of the principles laid down so many years ago in Geneva. The work of the two tribunals has considerably advanced those principles. The decisions handed down by the judges in trial and appeal chambers have begun to create a new international jurisprudence which, if allowed to develop further, will undoubtedly have a positive influence on national systems of law.

An important advance has been the considerable narrowing of the traditional and artificial distinction between international and internal wars. The appeals chamber of the Yugoslavia tribunal, in the *Tadić Jurisdiction Motion* case, made it clear that this distinction could no longer be sustained.[1] In the century that is about to end, millions of people have been killed, raped, tortured, or displaced as a result of internal wars. These wars are often brutal and have devastating effects upon civilian populations. As was held by the appeals chamber, it makes little sense to protect people from murder, rape, and wanton destruction of their property in the case of an international war but not to do so merely because the warring parties do not cross any international borders. The court emphasized that international humanitarian law is moving away from the traditional state-centered approach toward an international approach oriented toward human rights. Unfortunately, the provisions of the Rome Statute relating to war crimes appear to have revived the distinction.[2] Although murder and rape are equally prohibited in international and internal armed conflict by the Rome Statute, the provisions relating to destruction of property are more onerous in international armed conflict than in internal armed conflict.

A further important development is that the approach to mass rape has been significantly transformed by the recognition that such abhorrent conduct constitutes not only a war crime but also a crime against humanity. The tribunals are setting important precedents with respect to gender-related crimes, because this is the first time that systematic rape has ever been charged and prosecuted as a war crime in itself. In 1998, a trial chamber of the Rwanda tribunal handed down the first conviction for systematic rape as a war crime.

The tribunals have given rise to an international resurgence of humanitarian law. It is now written about and discussed daily in the media of many countries and is being taught with new interest in law schools. Perhaps most important, some political and military leaders in a number of countries are now paying attention to it. In 1996, when the Croatian government launched Operation Storm in the Krajina, Croatian leaders publicly exhorted their troops to protect civilians and not to violate international humanitarian law. These might be seen as small successes, but for the first time the law of war is present in the minds of some, if not all, political and military leaders who elect to make war. It must be conceded, however, that although the approach of the Serb forces in Kosovo has been significantly different from that of the Bosnian Serb ethnic cleansing in Bosnia, the slaughter of innocent civilians has in no way been averted by the existence of the International Criminal Tribunal for the former Yugoslavia. Robust support of the ICTY by the major Western nations and the arrests of Karadžić and Mladić, had they occurred, may have produced more respect for the tribunal and may have increased fear of apprehension and punishment.

One sees the serious interest that individual governments are taking in humanitarian law as a consequence of the tribunals. Three permanent members of the Security Council, the United States, France, and the United Kingdom, have passed national legislation recognizing their international obligation to comply with the statutes under which the United Nations tribunals operate. The Russian Federation formally informed the Yugoslavia tribunal that it does not require national legislation to do so and confirmed that it intended to comply with the provisions of the Security Council statute. Under tremendous international pressure, Croatia amended its Constitution to enable it to comply with the statute.

Another achievement of the tribunals has been to marginalize indicted war criminals who have not yet been arrested. Karadžić and Mladić, for example, have been removed from office for this very reason. But for his removal from office as president of the Republic of Srpska, Karadžić would have been able to attend the Dayton negotiations, and that would have kept the Bosnian government away. There would have been no Dayton agreement. And the indictment of Milošević will inevitably prevent the Federal Republic of Yugoslavia from joining the community of nations for as long as he remains the head of state.

In establishing the tribunals, the Security Council has struck a meaningful blow against impunity. It has sent out a message to would-be war criminals that the international community is no longer prepared to allow serious war crimes to be committed without the threat of retribution. The international community is in a stronger position than ever before to send this message. International humanitarian law has been substantially modified in the past fifty years to remove any obstacles that stood in the way of effective international policing. All this means that sovereignty, which was previously a state's best shield against any international intervention, is no longer absolute.

These exciting and important developments would not have occurred but for the energy and resolve of Madeleine Albright and her staff. David Scheffer played a key role in ensuring that the two United Nations tribunals were able to begin their work. Their support for all aspects of the work of the tribunals was impressive, and I hasten to add that at no time did anyone from the United States administration attempt to influence policy in the Office of the Prosecutor or impinge on its independence.

Since leaving the office of chief prosecutor, I have, to the best of my ability, remained in touch with events in The Hague and Arusha. I have had little contact with my successor and have avoided being privy to any confidential information. I wished to be free to speak out about the tribunals, and I could not have done so if I had knowledge of nonpublic information relating to the prosecutor's office. My main source of information has been the Internet and, in particular, the mass of information that comes to me daily from services such as Tribunal Watch and its successor, Just Watch.

I was delighted when I heard that President Clinton had nominated David Scheffer to be the special ambassador on war crimes. This was a demonstration of further support for the United Nations tribunals and also for an international criminal court. Again, the United States played a crucial role in having the General Assembly call an international diplomatic conference, which met in Rome during June and July 1998, to consider a treaty for the international criminal court. I had every confidence that the United States delegation to the Rome meeting would take the lead and help push the process to a successful conclusion. Alas, that is not what happened.

At the beginning of 1998, Morton Halperin, now head of policy at the State Department, and then director of the Twentieth Century Fund (now renamed the Century Foundation),[3] approached me to chair a task force of this fund comprising prominent Americans and Europeans who were pressing for the arrest of those indicted as war criminals by the Yugoslavia tribunal. I needed little persuasion to accept. Those who joined us included Robert Badinter, a former French minister of justice and now a member of the French Senate; Ted Meron, a professor of international law at New York University Law School and an adviser to me when I worked in The Hague; and Bianca Jagger, who has become a committed and vocal supporter of international justice. The task force held a number of meetings in Washington, D.C., and met with senior officials in the White House, the State Department, and the Pentagon. Whether through our efforts or not, during the second half of 1998, NATO adopted a more active policy, resulting in more arrests being made, most notably that of General Radislav Krstić, a senior Bosnian Serb army officer.

In his account of the Dayton negotiations, Richard Holbrooke frankly provides the following explanation for the failure to arrest Karadžić: "While the human-rights community and some members of the State Department, especially John Shattuck and Madeleine Albright, called for action, the military warned of casualties and Serb retaliation if an operation to arrest him took place. They said they would carry it out only if ordered to do so directly by the President; thus if anything went wrong the blame would fall on the civilians who had insisted on the operation, especially on the President himself. This was a heavy burden to lay on any president, particularly during an election year, and it was hardly surprising that no action was taken to mount, or even plan, an operation against Karadžić in 1996 or 1997." Holbrooke also explains how the Pentagon succeeded in keeping out of the Dayton Accords any obligation of the United Nations Implementing Force (IFOR) to arrest people, and how the commander of IFOR, Admiral Leighton Smith, was adamantly opposed to his troops going after indicted war criminals.[4]

I strongly believe that a decision on whether or not to arrest war criminals in Bosnia should have been made by the civilian authorities of the United States. It was, by definition, a political decision in which the advice of the military was clearly crucial. Nonetheless, the military should not have been allowed to veto a staunch policy concerning arrests and certainly should not have been allowed, in effect, to hold the president to ransom (whether or not it was an election year!).

I have no doubt that this same deference to the military caused the unfortunate approach of the United States administration at the Rome conference. At the heart of U.S. policy was the resolve that no international criminal court would be allowed to exercise jurisdiction over a United States citizen without the consent of the United States. For that reason Scheffer's team pushed for a provision whereby the prosecutor of the international criminal court would not be permitted to initiate any war crimes investigation without the consent of the Security Council. The United States veto would have been an effective shield against any investigation to which it objected. That the four other permanent members would have the same power to emasculate the prosecutor did not deter the United States from pushing for that provision. The stated fear of the United States was that some renegade or malicious prosecutor might some day initiate unfounded political prosecutions against United States citizens. The prospect of such conduct was made virtually impossible by the terms of the draft treaty. In the first place a prosecutor would have to have appropriate credentials and would be required to be elected by an absolute majority of the States Parties which, under the treaty, would have to comprise at least sixty nations that have ratified the treaty. Any decision by the prosecutor to initiate an investigation or to issue an indictment would have to be confirmed by a panel of three trial judges. The judges, in turn, whose specialist credentials are also set out in the treaty, would have to be elected by a majority of two-thirds of the members of the Assembly of States Parties. A further protection from unfounded prosecutions is to be found in what has been referred to as the system of complementarity. In terms of the treaty, the international criminal court has no jurisdiction over any person if the country of that person's citizenship has conducted a good-faith investigation into the alleged criminal conduct—whether or not there has been a conviction of that person. If the prosecutor alleges that the investigation or an ensuing trial was not conducted in good faith and was a sham, a trial chamber has to rule accordingly. And, in those proceedings, the country against which the allegation is made has standing to oppose the position of the prosecutor. I would add only that if the fears of the United States become a reality, the international criminal court would lose both credibility and the confidence and support of all decent nations.

Not surprisingly, these protective devices were sufficient to satisfy 120 members of the international community, including three permanent members of the Security Council, the United Kingdom, Russia, and France. The United States and six other nations, including China and Libya, opposed the treaty.

The Twentieth Century Fund Task Force decided to call a press conference during the first week of the Rome conference. We determined that with the eyes and ears of the world on Rome, it was a good opportunity to renew our call for the arrest of indicted war criminals. With the active support of Emma Bonino, European commissioner for human rights, the press conference was well attended and widely reported. I was also invited to address the plenary session of the conference on its third day. With only a five-minute slot, I had to prepare a short message. I concentrated on the moral obligations of the international community to the victims of war crimes. Unfortunately the victims are invariably at the bottom of the political agenda. I reminded the delegates that only by bringing justice to victims could there be any hope of avoiding calls for revenge and that their hate would sooner or later boil over into renewed violence. That was one of the lessons to be learned from the violence that has had such terrible consequences in both the former Yugoslavia and Rwanda.

During that week in Rome I had a private meeting with David Scheffer at the headquarters of the Food and Agriculture Organization, where the United Nations was hosting the diplomatic conference. We discussed some of the objections of the United States. The awkwardness of Scheffer's personal circumstances became apparent to me. Like most good advocates he appeared to have convinced himself of the justification of some of the arguments he had to support. But I know him sufficiently well to say, perhaps presumptuously, that he would have been far more comfortable had he been able to join with the overwhelming majority of delegations that were present.

The international criminal court will not begin its work until sixty nations have ratified the treaty. How long that will take is anybody's guess. Certainly a few years. What is not widely appreciated is that most nations will have to amend their own domestic laws substantially before they will be in a position to ratify the treaty. I did not appreciate the complexity of this aspect until recently, when I agreed to join a committee charged by the Cabinet with drafting a report on the laws that must be introduced or amended in order for the South African government to ratify the treaty. In the first place, to make the complementarity principle effective, it would be necessary to legislate for incorporation of the crimes defined in the treaty as domestic crimes, in particular genocide, crimes against humanity, and war crimes. Prison legislation would require that the government be authorized to imprison persons convicted and sentenced by the international criminal court. Legislation dealing with national intelligence would have to comply with the terms of the treaty. And provision would have to be made for the prosecutor and his or her staff to work in South Africa. This would include the right to interview witnesses and obtain assistance from relevant government agencies. One of the benefits of establishing the international criminal court is that governments, by going through this kind of exercise, are drawing attention to war crimes and mechanisms to prevent their commission.

There are important lessons to be learned from the United Nations War Crimes Tribunals:

- The complete and effective independence of the prosecutor is crucial. As is evident from my earlier discussions, if I had not had independence, both in fact and in perception, my work in South Africa, The Hague, and Arusha would seriously have been jeopardized — and so, too, the whole endeavor. By their nature, war crimes investigations are politically controversial, so that the independence of a war crimes prosecutor is even more important than that of prosecutors operating within national jurisdictions. I hasten to add that by upholding the independence of international prosecutors, I do not suggest that they not be held fully accountable for their actions. No public officer, regardless of his or her standing, should be exempt from public scrutiny. For that reason I am fully in favor of having the indictments of the ad hoc tribunals reviewed and confirmed by a trial judge. That judge, who will have received prejudicial evidence that might not subsequently be given by witnesses or relied on by the prosecution, may not participate in any proceedings flowing from the indictment, nor may any members of his or her chamber. The Rome Statute goes further and requires the prosecutor to obtain the permission of a pretrial chamber before investigations may begin. Review and confirmation of indictments are also required. Under the Rome Treaty system, too, the judges who sit on preliminary applications relating to investigations and review of indictments could not participate in any trial proceeding that might arise therefrom. The real point of independence is that the prosecutor should not be required to account to a political body for his or her policy or professional decisions. And, by the same token, a prosecutor should not have to take instructions from politicians on the exercise of prosecutorial discretion.

I concede that a prosecutor acting without regard to political reality may well cause problems and might interfere, for example, with a peace process. However, that risk is preferable to having politicians dictate to a prosecutor who should or should not be indicted and when indictments should be issued. In the case of Karadžić and

Mladić, for reasons given above, the views of Boutros-Ghali turned out to be incorrect. The point is that prosecutors cannot expect to be briefed fully on the politics of a situation, and politicians cannot expect to be briefed on the knowledge of the prosecutor.

- Ad hoc tribunals, such as those created by the Security Council for the former Yugoslavia and Bosnia, while better than nothing in the face of egregious war crimes, are an inefficient and politically unacceptable way of providing international justice. They are inefficient because they have to be developed from the ground up. With the best will in the world and without the sort of financial and bureaucratic problems I encountered, it would take not less than eighteen months to build an operating prosecutor's office and, in particular, an investigation department. Such delays are unacceptable and unfair to the victims of war crimes and also detract substantially from the deterrent value that justice might have in some situations. Ideally politics should not play a role in such humanitarian matters. The political wrangling that was associated with the appointment of a chief prosecutor for the Yugoslavia tribunal should not be allowed.

- It is unacceptable for a political body such as the Security Council to have the power of deciding where humanitarian law will or will not be enforced—the very issue the Serb minister of justice raised with me in Belgrade in October 1994.

- Renegade regimes must not be allowed to ignore the orders of an international court. This can only be avoided in the case of the international criminal court if the international community musters the political will to ensure that its orders are obeyed and that effective sanctions are introduced against any members who have ratified the treaty and renege on their obligations. It will also be necessary to visit pariah status upon any nations that persistently refuse to become parties to the treaty.

• The international character of the office of the chief prosecutor of the international criminal court is the best insurance that the policies adopted in that office will be professional and appropriate. Those not intimately associated with the Office of the Prosecutor do not realize that a dishonest or bad-faith agenda on the part of the chief prosecutor would quickly become public knowledge. When I left my office in The Hague in 1996, there were about 180 staff members, representing some forty countries on five continents. Many of them had been nominated by their governments. If we had adopted an anti-Serb or anti-Muslim stance, it would undoubtedly have been reported to concerned governments and to the media. Bear in mind, too, that in a professional office, all the policies are shared by all the people who work there. It was my practice to call regular staff meetings in order to give detailed reports on what we were doing and where we were going. The policies, in turn, were the consequence of the widest and most intense consultations. Daily meetings were held with the heads of each department so that each would know what the others were doing. In that atmosphere nothing of moment could have been kept secret for long. As was my experience with the South African commission, if colleagues are fully consulted and made part of the decision-making process, they respond with absolute loyalty and give their best.

The second half of the twentieth century has witnessed the proliferation of wars and war crimes. Huge areas such as the Great Lakes region of Central Africa have become destabilized, as more than a million people have been killed and many millions more have been forced to flee their homes with accompanying misery and hardship. In Rwanda there are tens of thousands of homes in which the eldest member of the family is a teenager. In Sierra Leone unimaginable atrocities were committed against innocent women, men, and children whose limbs were

amputated with machetes. For many decades the social and psychological problems these crimes have caused will retard the quest for
peace and security in these countries and regions. Ethnic cleansing
in the former Yugoslavia has resulted in a huge refugee population in
Europe, with more than three hundred thousand exiles in Germany
alone. Other examples abound. If this trend is not to continue into
the twenty-first century, then the international community will have
to take positive steps to arrest it. One effective deterrent would be an
international criminal justice system, sufficiently empowered to cause
would-be war criminals to reconsider their ambitions, knowing that
they might otherwise be hunted for the rest of their days and eventually be brought to justice. An overwhelming number of human rights
protagonists worldwide, including those in the United States, believe
that when the Rome Treaty is ratified by enough nations, a workable
and worthwhile court will be established. To say that the treaty could be
improved upon is implicit, but that is no reason to condemn it out of
hand.

Over the past fifty years the international community has become increasingly impatient with war crimes and war criminals. Nations that
disregard the fundamental human rights of their citizens no longer attempt to hide behind their national sovereignty when other nations or
international organizations interfere with and condemn their behavior. The death of apartheid is a dramatic example of that reality. As the
world contracts in consequence of modern technology, so the international community is able to exert more pressure on rogue governments
to respect fundamental human rights. What is required to encourage
and advance this welcome and healthy trend is the political will of the
most powerful nations. In that context, for the reasons I have discussed
in this chapter, the present stance of the United States is both disap-
pointing and regrettable. I am optimistic, however, that public opinion
in the United States will sooner or later impel the political leadership to

join the vast majority of nations and resume its leadership of the movement toward a more peaceful planet.

While I understand and sympathize with the frustration and even pessimism of human rights activists over the indifference of their political leaders, I am optimistic for the future of international justice. The advances in international law are beginning to have important consequences in areas of enforcement. I have already referred to the arrest of Pinochet. That has sent shock waves into the homes of other leaders who have violated the human rights of their people. During August 1999, General Momir Talić, one of the most senior Bosnian Serb army commanders, was attending a meeting in Vienna called by the Organization for Security and Cooperation in Europe (OSCE). He was called out of the meeting room to find Austrian police waiting to arrest him in terms of a warrant issued by the Yugoslavia tribunal. He had been secretly indicted for war crimes. Within hours he was in The Hague, where he is awaiting trial. Also in August 1999, Izzat Ibrahim al-Duri, regarded as Saddam Hussein's second-in-command, was in a Vienna hospital for treatment. Peter Pilz, a member of Vienna's city council, lodged a criminal complaint with the Austrian authorities, citing the mass murder of Kurds in 1988 and the murder and torture of other Iraqi citizens. Less than forty-eight hours later, Ibrahim made a hasty exit from Austria. Since then, he has presumably had to rely on hospitals in Iraq. These developments, according to press reports, also forced former President Suharto of Indonesia to forgo medical treatment in Germany. Other present and former dictators must be carefully reviewing their foreign travel plans.

The NATO bombing of the Federal Republic of Yugoslavia, in my view, will be seen historically as a watershed event. The armed might of the United States and west European nations was used in response to the human rights violations that the forces of Milošević were perpetrating against the Albanian population of Kosovo. So strongly did the

NATO members feel about these violations that they were prepared to take that unprecedented action, in apparent breach of the Charter of the United Nations, without the authority of the Security Council. They bypassed the Security Council to evade an inevitable Russian veto of such action. Never before had any nation used military force against a sovereign state for the sole reason that the human rights of its citizens were being violated. This was a new reliance on the universal jurisdiction in respect of egregious crimes.

In June 1999 I was approached by the prime minister of Sweden, Göran Persson, with the request that I head a new, independent international commission of inquiry into the events that have occurred in Kosovo. This Swedish initiative has the support of the governments of the United States, Russia, France, the United Kingdom, and Germany. The secretary-general of the United Nations, Kofi Annan, has also endorsed the appointment of this commission and has agreed to accept its report in September 2000. The American Bar Association, and in particular CEELI, has again been generous in making Mark Ellis available as the legal adviser to the commission. At its first meeting in Stockholm in September 1999, the commission defined its mandate in the following terms:

> The Independent International Commission on Kosovo will examine key developments prior to, during and after the Kosovo war, including systematic violations of human rights in the region.

> The Commission will present a detailed, objective analysis of the options that were available to the international community to cope with the crisis.

> It will focus on the origins of the Kosovo crisis, the diplomatic efforts to end the conflict, the role of the United Nations and NATO's decision to intervene militarily.

It will examine the resulting refugee crisis, including the responses of the international community to resolve the crisis. The effect of the conflict on regional and other states will also be examined.

Furthermore, the Commission will assess the role of humanitarian workers, NGOs and the media during the Kosovo war. Finally, the Commission will identify the norms of international law and diplomacy brought to the fore by the Kosovo war and the adequacy of present norms and institutions in preventing or responding to comparable crises in the future.[5]

Prior to World War II the victims of human rights abuses were not the subject of international concern. That has changed. No longer will dictators or oppressive governments be able to violate the fundamental rights of their citizens with impunity. We are moving into a new and different world, though as with all innovations there is initial discomfort and suspicion. I have no doubt, however, that the twenty-first century will witness the growth of an international criminal justice system and that victims of war crimes will no longer be ignored.

NOTES

Chapter 1: New Challenges

1. *S v Govender* 1986(3)SA 969 (T) at 971.
2. Walter Sisulu was an ANC leader and a co-accused of Mandela's at the trial, which resulted in their being sentenced to life imprisonment.
3. On 4 March 1985, the police opened fire on a large group of mourners proceeding to a funeral in Uitenhage. Twenty were killed.

Chapter 3: The South African Solution

1. The Open Society Foundation was established by George Soros, the New York financier and philanthropist. Under its umbrella, Open Society Funds have been set up in a number of new democracies, especially in central Europe. The foundation gives considerable sums to institutions of civil society that encourage openness and democracy.
2. *Dealing with the Past: Truth and Reconciliation in South Africa* (Cape Town: Institute for Democracy in South Africa, 1994), 118.
3. The cut-off date was initially earlier but was subsequently extended by Parliament.
4. *Azanian Peoples Organization (AZAPO) and Others v President of the Republic of South Africa and Others* 1996(4) SA 671 (CC).
5. José Zalaquett, "Balancing Ethical Imperatives and Political Con-

straints: The Dilemma of New Democracies Confronting Past Human Rights Violations," *Hastings Law Journal* 43, no. 6 (1992): 1438.

Chapter 4: International Justice

1. For more than three hundred years, piracy and brigandage have been recognized as crimes of universal jurisdiction. However, they were never authoritatively defined.
2. See Chapter 3.
3. Tadić, a local Bosnian Serb political leader, participated in the worst war crimes against inmates in the Omarska death camp, near the town of Prijedor.
4. Arthur Liman, *Lawyer Liman: A Life of Counsel and Controversy* (New York: Public Affairs, 1998), 309.
5. Richard Holbrooke, *To End a War* (New York: Random House, 1998), 219.

Chapter 5: Toward an International Criminal Court

1. Tadić placed in issue the authority of the Security Council to establish a war crimes tribunal. His complaint was dismissed by the trial and appeal chambers.
2. Article 8(2)(c) and (e) provide for violations that occur "in an armed conflict not of an international character."
3. A not-for-profit fund founded in 1919 and endowed by Edward A. Filene, the Century Foundation supervises analyses of economic policy, foreign affairs, and domestic political issues.
4. Holbrooke, *To End a War*, 338, 221, 339.
5. Press release, Kosovo Commission, Stockholm, 22 September 1999; see also www.kosovocommission.org.

GLOSSARY OF NAMES

LILLIAN BAQWA attorney and member of the Goldstone Commission

PROFUL BHAGWATI former chief justice of India

STEVE BIKO young leader of the Black Consciousness Movement who was murdered in police custody

GEORGE BIZOS senior counsel at the Johannesburg Bar; legal adviser to the Mandela family for more than thirty years

GRAHAM BLEWITT deputy prosecutor of the International Criminal Tribunal for the former Yugoslavia

ALEX BORAINE former opposition member of Parliament; national director of the Institute for a Democratic Alternative for South Africa (IDASA); deputy chairperson of the Truth and Reconciliation Commission

JOËLLE BOURGOIS former ambassador of France to South Africa

BOUTROS BOUTROS-GHALI secretary-general of the United Nations, 1992–96

PETER BRUCKNER former ambassador of Denmark to South Africa

ANTONIO CASSESE president of the International Criminal Tribunal for the Former Yugoslavia, 1993–97

ARTHUR CHASKALSON president of the Constitutional Court of South Africa

JACOBUS COETSEE minister of justice in South Africa, 1989–94

FREDERICK W. DE KLERK former president of the National Party; president of the Republic of South Africa, 1989–94

JOHAN DU TOIT deputy attorney-general of the Transvaal Province who led the evidence before the Sebokeng Commission; senior official of the Goldstone Commission; senior member of the Office of the Prosecutor at the International Criminal Tribunal for the former Yugoslavia

PETER HANSEN former counselor in the Danish Embassy in Pretoria

CONRAD HARPER former legal adviser to the U.S. State Department

PHILIP B. HEYMANN former deputy attorney-general of the United States; James Barr Ames Professor and director of the Center for Criminal Justice, Harvard University

PAUL KAGAMI deputy president of the Republic of Rwanda

RADOVAN KARADŽIĆ former president of the Republic of Srpska

WINNIE MADIKIZELA-MANDELA leading antiapartheid activist and former wife of Nelson Mandela

NELSON MANDELA former president of the African National Congress; president of the Republic of South Africa, 1994–99

ZINDZI MANDELA daughter of Nelson Mandela and Winnie Madikizela-Mandela

GILL MARCUS former spokesperson of the African National Congress; member of Parliament; deputy minister of finance; deputy governor of the South African Reserve Bank

SLOBODAN MILOŠEVIĆ president of the Federal Republic of Yugoslavia

RADKO MLADIĆ former commander of the Bosnian Serb Army

DULLAH OMAR minister of justice in South Africa, 1994–99

TORIE PRETORIUS director of the South African National Directorate of Prosecutions; member of the Goldstone Commission

ANTHONY REEVE former ambassador of the United Kingdom to South Africa

NEIL ROSSOUW former attorney general of the Cape Province; member of the Goldstone Commission

DAVID SCHEFFER United States ambassador at large for war crimes

CLAYTON SIZWE SITHOLE partner of Zindzi Mandela

SOLLY SITHOLE member of the Pretoria Bar and of the Goldstone Commission

GERT STEYN former president of the Port Elizabeth Regional Court; member of the Goldstone Commission

HELEN SUZMAN former opposition member of the South African Parliament; prominent member of the Progressive Federal Party and later the Democratic Party

DESMOND TUTU archbishop emeritus of Cape Town; chairperson of the Truth and Reconciliation Commission

CYRUS VANCE U.S. secretary of state in the Carter administration; representative of the secretary-general of the United Nations to South Africa, 1977–80, during the breakdown of transitional negotiations

P. A. J. WADDINGTON director of Criminal Justice Studies at the University of Reading, England

AKASHI YASUSHI former deputy secretary-general of the United Nations

INDEX